The American Presidency: A Very Short Introduction

VERY SHORT INTRODUCTIONS are for anyone wanting a stimulating and accessible way into a new subject. They are written by experts and have been translated into more than 40 different languages.

The series began in 1995 and now covers a wide variety of topics in every discipline. The VSI library now contains more than 450 volumes—a Very Short Introduction to everything from Indian philosophy to psychology and American history—and continues to grow in every subject area.

Very Short Introductions available now:

ACCOUNTING Christopher Nobes
ADOLESCENCE Peter K. Smith
ADVERTISING Winston Fletcher
AFRICAN AMERICAN RELIGION
    Eddie S. Glaude Jr
AFRICAN HISTORY John Parker and
    Richard Rathbone
AFRICAN RELIGIONS Jacob K. Olupona
AGNOSTICISM Robin Le Poidevin
AGRICULTURE Paul Brassley and
    Richard Soffe
ALEXANDER THE GREAT
    Hugh Bowden
ALGEBRA Peter M. Higgins
AMERICAN HISTORY Paul S. Boyer
AMERICAN IMMIGRATION
    David A. Gerber
AMERICAN LEGAL HISTORY
    G. Edward White
AMERICAN POLITICAL HISTORY
    Donald Critchlow
AMERICAN POLITICAL PARTIES
    AND ELECTIONS L. Sandy Maisel
AMERICAN POLITICS
    Richard M. Valelly
THE AMERICAN PRESIDENCY
    Charles O. Jones
THE AMERICAN REVOLUTION
    Robert J. Allison
AMERICAN SLAVERY
    Heather Andrea Williams
THE AMERICAN WEST Stephen Aron
AMERICAN WOMEN'S HISTORY
    Susan Ware

ANAESTHESIA Aidan O'Donnell
ANARCHISM Colin Ward
ANCIENT ASSYRIA Karen Radner
ANCIENT EGYPT Ian Shaw
ANCIENT EGYPTIAN ART AND
    ARCHITECTURE Christina Riggs
ANCIENT GREECE Paul Cartledge
THE ANCIENT NEAR EAST
    Amanda H. Podany
ANCIENT PHILOSOPHY Julia Annas
ANCIENT WARFARE Harry Sidebottom
ANGELS David Albert Jones
ANGLICANISM Mark Chapman
THE ANGLO-SAXON AGE John Blair
THE ANIMAL KINGDOM
    Peter Holland
ANIMAL RIGHTS David DeGrazia
THE ANTARCTIC Klaus Dodds
ANTISEMITISM Steven Beller
ANXIETY Daniel Freeman and
    Jason Freeman
THE APOCRYPHAL GOSPELS
    Paul Foster
ARCHAEOLOGY Paul Bahn
ARCHITECTURE Andrew Ballantyne
ARISTOCRACY William Doyle
ARISTOTLE Jonathan Barnes
ART HISTORY Dana Arnold
ART THEORY Cynthia Freeland
ASTROBIOLOGY David C. Catling
ASTROPHYSICS James Binney
ATHEISM Julian Baggini
AUGUSTINE Henry Chadwick
AUSTRALIA Kenneth Morgan

AUTISM Uta Frith
THE AVANT GARDE David Cottington
THE AZTECS David Carrasco
BACTERIA Sebastian G. B. Amyes
BARTHES Jonathan Culler
THE BEATS David Sterritt
BEAUTY Roger Scruton
BESTSELLERS John Sutherland
THE BIBLE John Riches
BIBLICAL ARCHAEOLOGY Eric H. Cline
BIOGRAPHY Hermione Lee
BLACK HOLES Katherine Blundell
THE BLUES Elijah Wald
THE BODY Chris Shilling
THE BOOK OF MORMON
    Terryl Givens
BORDERS Alexander C. Diener and
    Joshua Hagen
THE BRAIN Michael O'Shea
BRICS Andrew F. Cooper
THE BRITISH CONSTITUTION
    Martin Loughlin
THE BRITISH EMPIRE Ashley Jackson
BRITISH POLITICS Anthony Wright
BUDDHA Michael Carrithers
BUDDHISM Damien Keown
BUDDHIST ETHICS Damien Keown
BYZANTIUM Peter Sarris
CANCER Nicholas James
CAPITALISM James Fulcher
CATHOLICISM Gerald O'Collins
CAUSATION Stephen Mumford and
    Rani Lill Anjum
THE CELL Terence Allen and
    Graham Cowling
THE CELTS Barry Cunliffe
CHAOS Leonard Smith
CHEMISTRY Peter Atkins
CHILD PSYCHOLOGY Usha Goswami
CHILDREN'S LITERATURE
    Kimberley Reynolds
CHINESE LITERATURE Sabina Knight
CHOICE THEORY Michael Allingham
CHRISTIAN ART Beth Williamson
CHRISTIAN ETHICS D. Stephen Long
CHRISTIANITY Linda Woodhead
CITIZENSHIP Richard Bellamy
CIVIL ENGINEERING
    David Muir Wood
CLASSICAL LITERATURE William Allan

CLASSICAL MYTHOLOGY
    Helen Morales
CLASSICS Mary Beard and
    John Henderson
CLAUSEWITZ Michael Howard
CLIMATE Mark Maslin
CLIMATE CHANGE Mark Maslin
THE COLD WAR Robert McMahon
COLONIAL AMERICA Alan Taylor
COLONIAL LATIN AMERICAN
    LITERATURE Rolena Adorno
COMBINATORICS Robin Wilson
COMEDY Matthew Bevis
COMMUNISM Leslie Holmes
COMPLEXITY John H. Holland
THE COMPUTER Darrel Ince
COMPUTER SCIENCE
    Subrata Dasgupta
CONFUCIANISM Daniel K. Gardner
THE CONQUISTADORS
    Matthew Restall and
    Felipe Fernández-Armesto
CONSCIENCE Paul Strohm
CONSCIOUSNESS Susan Blackmore
CONTEMPORARY ART
    Julian Stallabrass
CONTEMPORARY FICTION
    Robert Eaglestone
CONTINENTAL PHILOSOPHY
    Simon Critchley
CORAL REEFS Charles Sheppard
CORPORATE SOCIAL
    RESPONSIBILITY Jeremy Moon
CORRUPTION Leslie Holmes
COSMOLOGY Peter Coles
CRIME FICTION Richard Bradford
CRIMINAL JUSTICE Julian V. Roberts
CRITICAL THEORY
    Stephen Eric Bronner
THE CRUSADES Christopher Tyerman
CRYPTOGRAPHY Fred Piper and
    Sean Murphy
CRYSTALLOGRAPHY A. M. Glazer
THE CULTURAL REVOLUTION
    Richard Curt Kraus
DADA AND SURREALISM
    David Hopkins
DANTE Peter Hainsworth and
    David Robey
DARWIN Jonathan Howard

THE DEAD SEA SCROLLS Timothy Lim
DECOLONIZATION Dane Kennedy
DEMOCRACY Bernard Crick
DERRIDA Simon Glendinning
DESCARTES Tom Sorell
DESERTS Nick Middleton
DESIGN John Heskett
DEVELOPMENTAL BIOLOGY
    Lewis Wolpert
THE DEVIL Darren Oldridge
DIASPORA Kevin Kenny
DICTIONARIES Lynda Mugglestone
DINOSAURS David Norman
DIPLOMACY Joseph M. Siracusa
DOCUMENTARY FILM
    Patricia Aufderheide
DREAMING J. Allan Hobson
DRUGS Leslie Iversen
DRUIDS Barry Cunliffe
EARLY MUSIC Thomas Forrest Kelly
THE EARTH Martin Redfern
EARTH SYSTEM SCIENCE Tim Lenton
ECONOMICS Partha Dasgupta
EDUCATION Gary Thomas
EGYPTIAN MYTH Geraldine Pinch
EIGHTEENTH-CENTURY BRITAIN
    Paul Langford
THE ELEMENTS Philip Ball
EMOTION Dylan Evans
EMPIRE Stephen Howe
ENGELS Terrell Carver
ENGINEERING David Blockley
ENGLISH LITERATURE Jonathan Bate
THE ENLIGHTENMENT
    John Robertson
ENTREPRENEURSHIP Paul Westhead
    and Mike Wright
ENVIRONMENTAL ECONOMICS
    Stephen Smith
ENVIRONMENTAL POLITICS
    Andrew Dobson
EPICUREANISM Catherine Wilson
EPIDEMIOLOGY Rodolfo Saracci
ETHICS Simon Blackburn
ETHNOMUSICOLOGY Timothy Rice
THE ETRUSCANS Christopher Smith
THE EUROPEAN UNION John Pinder
    and Simon Usherwood
EVOLUTION Brian and Deborah
    Charlesworth

EXISTENTIALISM Thomas Flynn
EXPLORATION Stewart A. Weaver
THE EYE Michael Land
FAMILY LAW Jonathan Herring
FASCISM Kevin Passmore
FASHION Rebecca Arnold
FEMINISM Margaret Walters
FILM Michael Wood
FILM MUSIC Kathryn Kalinak
THE FIRST WORLD WAR
    Michael Howard
FOLK MUSIC Mark Slobin
FOOD John Krebs
FORENSIC PSYCHOLOGY
    David Canter
FORENSIC SCIENCE Jim Fraser
FORESTS Jaboury Ghazoul
FOSSILS Keith Thomson
FOUCAULT Gary Gutting
THE FOUNDING FATHERS
    R. B. Bernstein
FRACTALS Kenneth Falconer
FREE SPEECH Nigel Warburton
FREE WILL Thomas Pink
FRENCH LITERATURE
    John D. Lyons
THE FRENCH REVOLUTION
    William Doyle
FREUD Anthony Storr
FUNDAMENTALISM Malise Ruthven
FUNGI Nicholas P. Money
GALAXIES John Gribbin
GALILEO Stillman Drake
GAME THEORY Ken Binmore
GANDHI Bhikhu Parekh
GENES Jonathan Slack
GENIUS Andrew Robinson
GEOGRAPHY John Matthews and
    David Herbert
GEOPOLITICS Klaus Dodds
GERMAN LITERATURE Nicholas Boyle
GERMAN PHILOSOPHY Andrew Bowie
GLOBAL CATASTROPHES Bill McGuire
GLOBAL ECONOMIC HISTORY
    Robert C. Allen
GLOBALIZATION Manfred Steger
GOD John Bowker
GOETHE Ritchie Robertson
THE GOTHIC Nick Groom
GOVERNANCE Mark Bevir

THE GREAT DEPRESSION AND THE NEW DEAL Eric Rauchway
HABERMAS James Gordon Finlayson
HAPPINESS Daniel M. Haybron
THE HARLEM RENAISSANCE Cheryl A. Wall
THE HEBREW BIBLE AS LITERATURE Tod Linafelt
HEGEL Peter Singer
HEIDEGGER Michael Inwood
HERMENEUTICS Jens Zimmermann
HERODOTUS Jennifer T. Roberts
HIEROGLYPHS Penelope Wilson
HINDUISM Kim Knott
HISTORY John H. Arnold
THE HISTORY OF ASTRONOMY Michael Hoskin
THE HISTORY OF CHEMISTRY William H. Brock
THE HISTORY OF LIFE Michael Benton
THE HISTORY OF MATHEMATICS Jacqueline Stedall
THE HISTORY OF MEDICINE William Bynum
THE HISTORY OF TIME Leofranc Holford-Strevens
HIV/AIDS Alan Whiteside
HOBBES Richard Tuck
HOLLYWOOD Peter Decherney
HORMONES Martin Luck
HUMAN ANATOMY Leslie Klenerman
HUMAN EVOLUTION Bernard Wood
HUMAN RIGHTS Andrew Clapham
HUMANISM Stephen Law
HUME A. J. Ayer
HUMOUR Noël Carroll
THE ICE AGE Jamie Woodward
IDEOLOGY Michael Freeden
INDIAN PHILOSOPHY Sue Hamilton
INFECTIOUS DISEASE Marta L. Wayne and Benjamin M. Bolker
INFORMATION Luciano Floridi
INNOVATION Mark Dodgson and David Gann
INTELLIGENCE Ian J. Deary
INTERNATIONAL LAW Vaughan Lowe
INTERNATIONAL MIGRATION Khalid Koser
INTERNATIONAL RELATIONS Paul Wilkinson

INTERNATIONAL SECURITY Christopher S. Browning
IRAN Ali M. Ansari
ISLAM Malise Ruthven
ISLAMIC HISTORY Adam Silverstein
ISOTOPES Rob Ellam
ITALIAN LITERATURE Peter Hainsworth and David Robey
JESUS Richard Bauckham
JOURNALISM Ian Hargreaves
JUDAISM Norman Solomon
JUNG Anthony Stevens
KABBALAH Joseph Dan
KAFKA Ritchie Robertson
KANT Roger Scruton
KEYNES Robert Skidelsky
KIERKEGAARD Patrick Gardiner
KNOWLEDGE Jennifer Nagel
THE KORAN Michael Cook
LANDSCAPE ARCHITECTURE Ian H. Thompson
LANDSCAPES AND GEOMORPHOLOGY Andrew Goudie and Heather Viles
LANGUAGES Stephen R. Anderson
LATE ANTIQUITY Gillian Clark
LAW Raymond Wacks
THE LAWS OF THERMODYNAMICS Peter Atkins
LEADERSHIP Keith Grint
LIBERALISM Michael Freeden
LIGHT Ian Walmsley
LINCOLN Allen C. Guelzo
LINGUISTICS Peter Matthews
LITERARY THEORY Jonathan Culler
LOCKE John Dunn
LOGIC Graham Priest
LOVE Ronald de Sousa
MACHIAVELLI Quentin Skinner
MADNESS Andrew Scull
MAGIC Owen Davies
MAGNA CARTA Nicholas Vincent
MAGNETISM Stephen Blundell
MALTHUS Donald Winch
MANAGEMENT John Hendry
MAO Delia Davin
MARINE BIOLOGY Philip V. Mladenov
THE MARQUIS DE SADE John Phillips
MARTIN LUTHER Scott H. Hendrix
MARTYRDOM Jolyon Mitchell

MARX Peter Singer
MATERIALS Christopher Hall
MATHEMATICS Timothy Gowers
THE MEANING OF LIFE Terry Eagleton
MEDICAL ETHICS Tony Hope
MEDICAL LAW Charles Foster
MEDIEVAL BRITAIN John Gillingham
  and Ralph A. Griffiths
MEDIEVAL LITERATURE
  Elaine Treharne
MEDIEVAL PHILOSOPHY
  John Marenbon
MEMORY Jonathan K. Foster
METAPHYSICS Stephen Mumford
THE MEXICAN REVOLUTION
  Alan Knight
MICHAEL FARADAY
  Frank A. J. L. James
MICROBIOLOGY Nicholas P. Money
MICROECONOMICS Avinash Dixit
MICROSCOPY Terence Allen
THE MIDDLE AGES Miri Rubin
MINERALS David Vaughan
MODERN ART David Cottington
MODERN CHINA Rana Mitter
MODERN DRAMA
  Kirsten E. Shepherd-Barr
MODERN FRANCE
  Vanessa R. Schwartz
MODERN IRELAND Senia Pašeta
MODERN JAPAN
  Christopher Goto-Jones
MODERN LATIN AMERICAN
  LITERATURE
  Roberto González Echevarría
MODERN WAR Richard English
MODERNISM Christopher Butler
MOLECULES Philip Ball
THE MONGOLS Morris Rossabi
MOONS David A. Rothery
MORMONISM Richard Lyman Bushman
MOUNTAINS Martin F. Price
MUHAMMAD Jonathan A. C. Brown
MULTICULTURALISM Ali Rattansi
MUSIC Nicholas Cook
MYTH Robert A. Segal
THE NAPOLEONIC WARS
  Mike Rapport
NATIONALISM Steven Grosby
NELSON MANDELA Elleke Boehmer

NEOLIBERALISM Manfred Steger and
  Ravi Roy
NETWORKS Guido Caldarelli and
  Michele Catanzaro
THE NEW TESTAMENT
  Luke Timothy Johnson
THE NEW TESTAMENT AS
  LITERATURE Kyle Keefer
NEWTON Robert Iliffe
NIETZSCHE Michael Tanner
NINETEENTH-CENTURY BRITAIN
  Christopher Harvie and
  H. C. G. Matthew
THE NORMAN CONQUEST
  George Garnett
NORTH AMERICAN INDIANS
  Theda Perdue and Michael D. Green
NORTHERN IRELAND
  Marc Mulholland
NOTHING Frank Close
NUCLEAR PHYSICS Frank Close
NUCLEAR POWER Maxwell Irvine
NUCLEAR WEAPONS
  Joseph M. Siracusa
NUMBERS Peter M. Higgins
NUTRITION David A. Bender
OBJECTIVITY Stephen Gaukroger
THE OLD TESTAMENT
  Michael D. Coogan
THE ORCHESTRA D. Kern Holoman
ORGANIZATIONS Mary Jo Hatch
PAGANISM Owen Davies
THE PALESTINIAN-ISRAELI
  CONFLICT Martin Bunton
PARTICLE PHYSICS Frank Close
PAUL E. P. Sanders
PEACE Oliver P. Richmond
PENTECOSTALISM William K. Kay
THE PERIODIC TABLE Eric R. Scerri
PHILOSOPHY Edward Craig
PHILOSOPHY IN THE ISLAMIC
  WORLD Peter Adamson
PHILOSOPHY OF LAW
  Raymond Wacks
PHILOSOPHY OF SCIENCE
  Samir Okasha
PHOTOGRAPHY Steve Edwards
PHYSICAL CHEMISTRY Peter Atkins
PILGRIMAGE Ian Reader
PLAGUE Paul Slack

PLANETS David A. Rothery
PLANTS Timothy Walker
PLATE TECTONICS Peter Molnar
PLATO Julia Annas
POLITICAL PHILOSOPHY
    David Miller
POLITICS Kenneth Minogue
POSTCOLONIALISM Robert Young
POSTMODERNISM Christopher Butler
POSTSTRUCTURALISM Catherine Belsey
PREHISTORY Chris Gosden
PRESOCRATIC PHILOSOPHY
    Catherine Osborne
PRIVACY Raymond Wacks
PROBABILITY John Haigh
PROGRESSIVISM Walter Nugent
PROTESTANTISM Mark A. Noll
PSYCHIATRY Tom Burns
PSYCHOANALYSIS Daniel Pick
PSYCHOLOGY Gillian Butler and
    Freda McManus
PSYCHOTHERAPY Tom Burns and
    Eva Burns-Lundgren
PURITANISM Francis J. Bremer
THE QUAKERS Pink Dandelion
QUANTUM THEORY
    John Polkinghorne
RACISM Ali Rattansi
RADIOACTIVITY Claudio Tuniz
RASTAFARI Ennis B. Edmonds
THE REAGAN REVOLUTION Gil Troy
REALITY Jan Westerhoff
THE REFORMATION Peter Marshall
RELATIVITY Russell Stannard
RELIGION IN AMERICA Timothy Beal
THE RENAISSANCE Jerry Brotton
RENAISSANCE ART
    Geraldine A. Johnson
REVOLUTIONS Jack A. Goldstone
RHETORIC Richard Toye
RISK Baruch Fischhoff and John Kadvany
RITUAL Barry Stephenson
RIVERS Nick Middleton
ROBOTICS Alan Winfield
ROMAN BRITAIN Peter Salway
THE ROMAN EMPIRE
    Christopher Kelly
THE ROMAN REPUBLIC
    David M. Gwynn
ROMANTICISM Michael Ferber

ROUSSEAU Robert Wokler
RUSSELL A. C. Grayling
RUSSIAN HISTORY Geoffrey Hosking
RUSSIAN LITERATURE Catriona Kelly
THE RUSSIAN REVOLUTION
    S. A. Smith
SAVANNA Peter A. Furley
SCHIZOPHRENIA Chris Frith and
    Eve Johnstone
SCHOPENHAUER
    Christopher Janaway
SCIENCE AND RELIGION Thomas Dixon
SCIENCE FICTION David Seed
THE SCIENTIFIC REVOLUTION
    Lawrence M. Principe
SCOTLAND Rab Houston
SEXUALITY Véronique Mottier
SHAKESPEARE'S COMEDIES
    Bart van Es
SIKHISM Eleanor Nesbitt
THE SILK ROAD James A. Millward
SLANG Jonathon Green
SLEEP Steven W. Lockley and
    Russell G. Foster
SOCIAL AND CULTURAL
    ANTHROPOLOGY
    John Monaghan and Peter Just
SOCIAL PSYCHOLOGY Richard J. Crisp
SOCIAL WORK Sally Holland and
    Jonathan Scourfield
SOCIALISM Michael Newman
SOCIOLINGUISTICS John Edwards
SOCIOLOGY Steve Bruce
SOCRATES C. C. W. Taylor
SOUND Mike Goldsmith
THE SOVIET UNION Stephen Lovell
THE SPANISH CIVIL WAR
    Helen Graham
SPANISH LITERATURE Jo Labanyi
SPINOZA Roger Scruton
SPIRITUALITY Philip Sheldrake
SPORT Mike Cronin
STARS Andrew King
STATISTICS David J. Hand
STEM CELLS Jonathan Slack
STRUCTURAL ENGINEERING
    David Blockley
STUART BRITAIN John Morrill
SUPERCONDUCTIVITY
    Stephen Blundell

SYMMETRY Ian Stewart
TAXATION Stephen Smith
TEETH Peter S. Ungar
TERRORISM Charles Townshend
THEATRE Marvin Carlson
THEOLOGY David F. Ford
THOMAS AQUINAS Fergus Kerr
THOUGHT Tim Bayne
TIBETAN BUDDHISM
    Matthew T. Kapstein
TOCQUEVILLE Harvey C. Mansfield
TRAGEDY Adrian Poole
THE TROJAN WAR Eric H. Cline
TRUST Katherine Hawley
THE TUDORS John Guy
TWENTIETH-CENTURY BRITAIN
    Kenneth O. Morgan
THE UNITED NATIONS
    Jussi M. Hanhimäki

THE U.S. CONGRESS Donald A. Ritchie
THE U.S. SUPREME COURT
    Linda Greenhouse
UTOPIANISM Lyman Tower Sargent
THE VIKINGS Julian Richards
VIRUSES Dorothy H. Crawford
WATER John Finney
THE WELFARE STATE David Garland
WILLIAM SHAKESPEARE
    Stanley Wells
WITCHCRAFT Malcolm Gaskill
WITTGENSTEIN A. C. Grayling
WORK Stephen Fineman
WORLD MUSIC Philip Bohlman
THE WORLD TRADE
    ORGANIZATION Amrita Narlikar
WORLD WAR II Gerhard L. Weinberg
WRITING AND SCRIPT
    Andrew Robinson

Available soon:

LEARNING Mark Haselgrove
BLOOD Chris Cooper
TRANSLATION Matthew Reynolds

PUBLIC HEALTH Virginia Berridge
INDIAN CINEMA
    Ashish Rajadhyaksha

For more information visit our web site

www.oup.com/vsi/

Charles O. Jones

THE AMERICAN PRESIDENCY

A Very Short Introduction

Second Edition

OXFORD
UNIVERSITY PRESS

OXFORD
UNIVERSITY PRESS

Oxford University Press is a department of the
University of Oxford. It furthers the University's objective
of excellence in research, scholarship, and education
by publishing worldwide. Oxford is a registered trade mark of Oxford
University Press in the UK and certain other countries.

Published in the United States of America by Oxford University Press
198 Madison Avenue, New York, NY 10016, United States of America

Library of Congress Cataloging-in-Publication Data
Names: Jones, Charles O., author.
Title: The American Presidency : a very short introduction / Charles O. Jones.
Description: Second edition. | New York, NY : Oxford University Press, 2016.
| Series: Very short introductions | Includes index.
Identifiers: LCCN 2015044422 | ISBN 9780190458201 (paperback)
Subjects: LCSH: Presidents—United States. | Executive power—United States.
| BISAC: POLITICAL SCIENCE / Government /
Executive Branch. | HISTORY /
United States / General.
Classification: LCC JK516 .J636 2016 | DDC 352.230973—dc23
LC record available at http://lccn.loc.gov/2015044422

3 5 7 9 8 6 4 2

Printed in Great Britain
by Ashford Colour Press Ltd., Gosport, Hants.
on acid-free paper

Contents

List of illustrations   xiii

Preface   xv

Acknowledgments   xvii

1   Inventing the presidency   1

2   The presidency finds its place   23

3   Electing presidents (and other ways to occupy the Oval Office)   42

4   Making and remaking a presidency   67

5   Connecting to and leading the government   85

6   Presidents at work: making law and doing policy   109

7   Reform, change, and prospects for the future   142

Appendix: Presidents and Vice Presidents of the United States of America   167

References   173

Further reading   175

Index   179

List of illustrations

1. Howard Chandler Christy's
    *Signing of the
    Constitution.* **6**
    Architect of the Capitol,
    AOC no. 70242

2. Major L'Enfant's design for
    the "Federal City." **25**
    Library of Congress, Prints and
    Photographs Division, Historic
    American Buildings Survey,
    National Park Service, DC668

3. President Obama delivering
    the State of the Union
    message, 2013. **33**
    Official White House Photo by
    Pete Souza

4. President Bill Clinton's
    inauguration, January 20,
    1993. **62**
    Architect of the Capitol,
    AOC no. 73564

5. President Reagan with his
    cabinet. **71**

    National Archives and Records
    Administration (ARC 198576)

6. President Eisenhower and
    President-elect Kennedy. **76**
    Dwight D. Eisenhower Library

7. White House, West Wing
    floor plan. **98**
    GlobalSecurity.org

8. President George W. Bush
    campaigning for support. **115**
    US Air Force photo by Staff Sgt.
    Jim Verchio

9. President Johnson signs
    Medical Care for the Aged Act
    of 1965. **128**
    LBJ Library photo by Yoichi R.
    Okamoto (A985-6a)

10. President Roosevelt's joint
    press conference with Prime
    Minister Churchill. **159**
    AP Photo

Preface

I am, at this writing, living with my fourteenth president—from Herbert Hoover to Barack H. Obama. I don't remember much of anything about Hoover, though my midwestern family talked about him rather proudly because he came from Iowa. I have strong personal and scholarly impressions of the rest. I recall the day in 1944 when I came to live in Canton, South Dakota, with my grandparents. I was sporting an FDR button. My grandfather made me take it off. He liked Truman even less, though my grandfather's plainspoken style reminded me of Truman. Put it this way: Had they met, they would have understood each other.

I paid attention to presidents through my school and college years, wondering how you got to be one. Having had FDR as my first impression, and in spite of my grandfather, I thought they were superhuman. Later I learned it was the expectations that were beyond human. And so I have watched presidents pass through, fascinated by their efforts to manage responsibilities well enough to receive credit for the good as ballast for the certainty of blame for the bad.

The management of disproportionate and often conflicting expectations is the theme of this book. Quite remarkably, the urges that were present in Philadelphia at the writing of the Constitution are still evident today. We want to hold presidents accountable for what happens in government, but we don't want them to have too much power. So we hedge our bets all around by granting powers, then checking, balancing, and sharing them.

It would be fair to hold the system responsible and all those who make it work over time and across issues. After all, presidents are in-and-outers, seldom getting all they want, and much of what happens is a result of actions by others (including previous administrations). Trouble is, a system isn't individual or personal, and so it is hard to say who is at fault when things go bad. Yet it is precisely then that we typically want accountability. And so there they are, the presidents as chief executives, the names we all learn. It is their time of accountability—we even mark our political eras with their names: the Roosevelt, Eisenhower, or Clinton years.

I strive in this Very Short Introduction to portray the challenges of presidential leadership in a separated powers system. Executive accountability is a part of that system—it goes with the job. Members of Congress answer to different voting publics; judges respond to the law and the precedents set by their decisions. It was by no means certain the system would last, but it has. I have endeavored to explain why and to contribute to understanding how.

Charles O. Jones
Wintergreen, Virginia

Acknowledgments

I am indebted to the many scholars, journalists, and politicians who have, over the years, taught me about the presidency. The list is too long to include here. It is no surprise, however, that Dick Neustadt heads the list. Those familiar with his work will spot its influence in these pages.

Given the purpose of this series, I asked a few nonexpert, politically aware friends and neighbors to react to my original proposal. The comments of David and Georgia Orphan, Bob and Kathy Knowles, Lou and Toni Jones, Reg Hall, and Vera Jones were very helpful, full of common sense suggestions that I followed to the letter. Three anonymous scholarly reviewers also provided useful reactions to the proposal.

Kate Hamill, then at Oxford University Press, worked with me to refine the proposal further, as well as to reassure me that the project was worth doing. Dedi Felman took over as the editor once the chapters were written. She has a remarkable capacity to spot what can be done better and to estimate an author's skill for achieving more. Her editorial nudgings were consistently on target, substantially improving the manuscript.

Others at Oxford University Press were also helpful in overseeing the production of the book. Michele Bové searched for and found appropriate pictures, in addition to managing the transformation of manuscript to book. Each stage was skillfully handled and for that I am most appreciative.

The book is dedicated to my remarkably talented sisters and brothers. I am forever grateful for their love, support, and good humor. Fact is, we are a very funny (all meanings) group in a somewhat less than amusing world.

For this edition thanks to Nancy Toff, who asked me to revise my book. She guided the revision throughout—advising, editing, reviewing illustrations, managing production. She is, among many fine attributes, an email responder, frequently at night from home. Remarkable. I am as grateful as any author can be for her professional capabilities and her good nature. Joellyn Ausanka and Claudia Dukeshire oversaw the copyediting process and other details; Mary Sutherland improved the text with her careful copy editing.

Chapter 1
Inventing the presidency

Imagine being present at the founding of a nation. Who will have powers? How will those with powers be chosen? Will there be one leader or many? How will the government be organized? Will it last? These and other questions faced James Madison, Benjamin Franklin, Alexander Hamilton, and George Washington, among the most illustrious political thinkers and practitioners of public affairs at the time.

Not willing to repeat the governing errors made by others in those days, the Founders looked for new answers. That quest explains why it would have been so exhilarating to be in attendance. The creative work of this group in writing the Constitution of the United States in Philadelphia in the summer of 1787 has been interpreted and invoked regularly in political and policy debate for more than two centuries.

The first founding, a weak confederation ratified in 1781, had failed. Six years later, anxious politicians recognized the faults and met to design a more workable government before it was too late. Their gathering was like no other. It produced a unique plan, one applied ultimately to vast regions across a continent. Seldom in history had conditions been so favorable for institutional innovation.

Among the most experimental creations was that of the presidency itself. It was generally understood that more effective leadership for the government was required. But could that goal be achieved while sufficient checks were maintained to prevent tyranny? The ultimate aim was, therefore, to govern, not merely to control, and the solution was the separation of powers. Presidents would live and work within a constitutional construction that divvied up powers in order to promote and preserve unity.

Think about it: *separating to unify*. Pondering that aphorism will enhance your admiration for what was undertaken and accomplished in Philadelphia, not to mention providing a basis for understanding American government and politics. The urge to protect the populace from tyranny was strong, thus the emphasis on dividing power. Yet the parts had to unite sufficiently for governing, doing so as representative institutions. The design had to be as special as the purpose, with each person and faction subject to checks and sensitive to balance by others. It was a bold and noble experiment, one still being tested.

The word "presidency" cannot be found in the Constitution. That label was affixed to the executive department of the government only later. There were executives called "presidents" at the time. New Hampshire and Pennsylvania had them, as did South Carolina. Those chairing the Continental Congress and the Constitutional Convention itself were called "presidents," as was the delegate chosen to preside over the Committee of States under the Articles of Confederation. But these were not "presidencies" as the term came to be used to designate an institution of executive powers and functions.

Why the title "president"? Why not "governor," the more common title among the states? The answer reveals a basic dilemma facing the Founders. Americans were understandably wary of executive powers as exercised by the King of England. In fact, the first government under the Articles of Confederation had no executive branch as such. Yet it was generally agreed in Philadelphia that one was needed for more effective governance. The title of "governor" was proposed at different times in Philadelphia but the title was commonly used in the colonies for the unpopular heads appointed by English royalty. The title "president" was more neutral, possibly less commanding, deriving as it does from *praesidere*, essentially "to preside." And that is how the presidents of the Constitutional Convention and the Continental and Confederation Congresses served; they presided.

"President" it would be then, suiting the need for an executive title both nonthreatening and uplifting. After experiencing other forms, from English rule to an executiveless Confederation, a mostly new title for the head of state marked a fresh start. The debates over the executive's reach and status in the separated system had, however, just begun. All presidents have pondered their place in the national government precisely because it was never explicitly set forth. Each has had to devise means to comprehend and meet the critical challenge: how to promote unity in a separated system.

George Washington: the founding presider

If faced with developing a positive impression of executive power, one could hardly wish for more than a George Washington as the first president. He might have been called "George the Reluctant" for the number of times that he had expressed a preference for staying in his home at Mount Vernon rather than serving in top leadership positions. His reluctance seemingly made him even more desirable, especially given the disputes among those who did yearn to serve.

There he sat, presiding over the Constitutional Convention, his very presence offering reassurance that each increment of power vested in the president would be judiciously exercised. Pierce

3

Butler, delegate from South Carolina, explained that the president's powers would not "have been so great had not many of the members cast their eyes toward General Washington as President: and shaped their ideas of the Powers to be given to a President, by their opinions of his Virtue." He was the general who defeated the British and then went home. "His Excellency" was not a designation he would invite. And, in fact, when a committee included that title in its report to the Convention on August 6, 1787, a motion was made and passed to have it removed.

The prospect that Washington would be the nation's first president also reinforced the Convention's steady progress toward equal status and independence of the branches. Early proposals were weighted toward a prevailing Congress to include having the executive chosen by that body. The weakness of the Articles of Confederation had, however, amply demonstrated the need for an executive with status independent of the legislature, perhaps by separate election. Washington's character and personality facilitated styling the presidency as an office not beholden to Congress, thus contributing to the development of a government of separated powers.

At the creation

Most people have had experiences in governing—for example, by being on a school board, in a business group, labor union, charity board, or condo association (very nasty politics that). Therefore, had you been at the Constitutional Convention, it would not have surprised you to see committees formed. They serve such critical functions: defusing contentious issues (or discovering they cannot be resolved), refining proposals, identifying effects, and integrating ideas. The most pronounced views at the Constitutional Convention were those of the Anti-Federalists, who were mostly content to make corrections to the Articles of Confederation, and the Federalists, who wanted a strengthened central government of real authority. The views and recommendations of these two factions were incorporated into two plans offered to the delegates. The New Jersey plan was little more than a revision of the Articles; the Virginia Plan aimed to create a more powerful national government. Neither was as bold as the final document, a point revealing the fascinating and creative dynamics of the meeting.

Critical to any restructuring was establishing an independently elected executive. Embedded in that issue was whether there would indeed be a separation of powers. Therefore, forming what would become the presidency was deliberate and deliberative. For as Alexander Hamilton later wrote in *Federalist No. 67*: "There is hardly any part of the system which could have been attended with greater difficulty in the arrangements of it than this [the executive department]; and there is, perhaps, none that has been inveighed against with less candor or more criticized with less judgment."

The evidence for the heated exchanges alluded to in Hamilton's observation can be found in the series of decisions culminating in Article II, which deals with the executive. The Convention went back and forth on fundamental issues regarding executive selection and powers. Why? Forming legislatures and courts was familiar work for those several Framers and their friends who had been involved in writing or serving under state constitutions. The assembled were less acquainted with how to create a separate, independent, consequential, yet forbearing executive. Several delegates were fearful of going too far in allocating powers to the executive, understanding there would be presidents to follow Washington who might not be as reluctant to seek or exploit those powers. In fact, even those Federalists supporting a strong central government originally provided in the Virginia Plan for the executive to be chosen by Congress.

Work on the presidency at the Convention progressed from an executive selected and constrained by Congress to one

1. Signing the Constitution in Philadelphia, September 17, 1787, George Washington presiding.

independently elected and possessed of significant domestic and foreign policy authority. The principal issues in the debate over the executive were selection, one executive or more, term length, succession, removal, and powers. All were vital, but the matter of selection determined the separation of powers since a president elected by Congress could not truly be separate from that branch.

Selection

It was not until September that the Convention agreed to the independent election of the executive. The Virginia and New Jersey plans both proposed having the executive elected by the legislature. The Virginia Plan provided for a two-house, or bicameral, legislature, the New Jersey Plan for a one-house, or unicameral, legislature.

Selection by a bicameral legislature was included in the report of the Committee of the Whole on June 13, and later in the report of the Committee of Detail on August 6. No particulars on balloting were included in either report. The Committee of Detail report simply stated "His Excellency" [the title proposed for the president] "shall be elected by ballot by the Legislature." One might have thought the election of an "Excellency" deserved a bit more detail.

Having the executive elected by the legislature would have resulted in a parliamentary system once political parties were formed. Whichever party, or coalition of parties or factions, was in the majority would likely have selected one of their own to serve as president. The United States would then have been governed by a unitary, not a separated, system. That is, one branch, the legislature, would choose the leader of another, the executive. At the least, the separation of powers requires the separation of executive and legislative elections.

Election by the legislature was approved at first, primarily as a point of departure. Still, the delegates were divided on the issue between those wary of an independent executive (the Anti-Federalists) and those preferring a strengthened executive (the Federalists). The first group favored legislative election; the second favored a popular vote or electors chosen for the purpose of selecting an executive. The matter was so divisive and the subsidiary issues so interwoven (for example, term length and succession) that the final resolution was left to the Committee on Postponed Matters. As it happened, those favoring an independent executive had a majority on the committee, and the Electoral College was born. Popular election of the president never had sufficient support among the delegates and so another system had to be found, essentially a hybrid incorporating legislative and state interests.

The Electoral College system perplexes many Americans and virtually all foreigners. However, it was not designed to confuse (although the reason an institution with neither faculty or students was designated a "College" is not exactly clear). The proposal was a masterful attempt to meld and satisfy contending points of view. The legislature would have bearing on the presidential election in two important ways: The number of electors for a state would be equal to the number of representatives allocated to the state on the basis of population plus two for its senators; and the House of Representatives, voting as states, not individuals, would choose the president should no one candidate receive a majority of electoral votes. The Senate, voting as individuals, not states, would choose the vice president under those circumstances. Finally, the states would determine how electors would be appointed, including the option of their being popularly elected.

The plan was approved at the Convention by nine states to two (voting was by states, not individual delegates), the same count that had initially favored presidential election by the legislature, a remarkable turnaround in the delegates' thinking. Thus it was that the separation of powers was fixed in the Constitution by dividing the elections of the legislature and the executive. As it has developed in practice, presidential candidates have campaigned nationally to gain a majority of electors, and members of the Senate and the House have campaigned in the states and congressional districts. Consequently, what a president proposed would be screened by lawmakers representing individually based constituency interests. The outcome is three interdependent national readings of the voting public: one each by the results for president, senators, and representatives. It is this representational mix that produces national laws or prevents their enactment.

One or more

The government of the Articles of Confederation provided that "a Committee of the States," with one delegate from each state, would be responsible "for managing the general affairs of the united states." One of the delegates was to be appointed "president" to serve no longer than one year in any term of three years. The limitation of this arrangement—a president with severely limited tenure working with an executive committee—was a primary motivation for constitutional change. Therefore, in designing more effective management of "general affairs," the Convention had to consider whether to have one executive or a committee or council.

Given the failures of the government under the Articles and the weakness of most executive arrangements in the states, it was surprising that any of the delegates supported a plural executive. But the most senior delegate in age, Benjamin Franklin, was an advocate, having supported a twelve-person executive council in his state of Pennsylvania. John Dickinson from Delaware also favored a three-person executive, one each for the northeastern, middle, and southern states. And the New Jersey plan provided for congressional election of a plural executive (number unspecified).

A motion for a single executive was debated very early in the proceedings and passed, seven states to three, on June 4. Thereafter the issue would not be seriously revisited. However the executive was to be elected, however long the term in office, and whatever the eligibility for succession, the executive department would be headed by a single person.

Term length and renewal

How long should the single executive serve? Four years now seems obvious, but that term came to the delegates quite late in the proceedings. And should the person be term limited? These were contentious issues at the Convention, as they were allied with the very essence of executive powers in the new government. Hamilton, who wrote most of the *Federalist* essays, explained the advantages of longer terms in *No. 71*: "It is a general principle of human nature, that a man will be interested in whatever he possesses, in proportion to the firmness or precariousness of the tenure by which he holds it; will be less attached to what he holds by a momentary or uncertain title, than to what he enjoys by a durable or certain title; and, of course, will be willing to risk more for the sake of the one, than for the other." Yet, while durable, an executive elected for a long term bore the features of life-serving monarchs whom most Americans despised. Therefore, the longer the term, the more likely it was that the executive would not be eligible to serve again.

There was reluctance on this issue to emulate either the states or the Articles of Confederation. Annual election was typical in both, often including a form of term limitation (for example, having to wait for a period of years—the number varied—before serving again). Most delegates agreed that one year of service was too short, but those most fearful of a strong central government, the Anti-Federalists, were also dubious about permitting renewal regardless of the length of the term in office. Why? Because some states with one-year terms and reeligibility had governors reelected over and over again. In New York, with three-year terms, voters reelected George Clinton six times. Such a case raised concerns about a president for life.

It was not surprising that several proposals for term length and renewal were offered in Philadelphia. Lacking historical practice with different term lengths, one person's estimate as to what would work well was as good as another's. Early in the proceedings it was agreed that the executive should serve a single seven-year term. Ineligibility for a second term was subsequently removed, then reinserted in late July.

Uncertainty about what was best led to delegates' changing their minds along the way. I picture the debate on this subject as a kind of term-length auction: "I have six years. Do I hear seven? Seven years? Six and a half?" At different times there were proposals for a renewable six years; single eight-, eleven-, fifteen-, and twenty-year terms; for no more than six years' service in twelve; and during good behavior (essentially a life term for the well comported). Many delegates participated in the numbers game. Given the disparate proposals and uncertain effects, the issues of term length and renewal were sent off to the Committee on Postponed Matters, a convenient and useful means for settling matters not resolvable in full session.

The Committee settled on four years, a shorter term than had heretofore been proposed but with no restrictions on eligibility for second or subsequent terms. The plan was a victory for those favoring a strong executive and, hence, was criticized during the ratification debates in the states as inviting the corruption of electors in the Electoral College by an executive anxious to serve for life.

As it happened in practice, George Washington helped immeasurably to allay these fears. He declined to serve a third term in 1796, thus seemingly introducing a two-term limit, one not broken until 1940 when Franklin D. Roosevelt (FDR) ran for a third term, and again in 1944, for a fourth. In 1951, the Twenty-second Amendment, limiting the president to two terms, was ratified. Henceforth Washington's precedent was officially a part of the Constitution.

Removal

In 1998 the American people learned about impeachment. In accordance with procedures set forth in the Constitution, President Bill Clinton was impeached by the House of Representatives. Subsequently, he was tried and acquitted by the Senate. The Chief Justice of the United States, William H. Rehnquist, presided over the Senate trial.

Several of those supporting the president in 1998–99 questioned the propriety of the accusers, asserting they were, in essence, seeking to nullify Clinton's reelection in 1996. It was an argument reminiscent of Alexander Hamilton's summary of the issues involved in impeaching a president as set forth in *Federalist No. 65*: "A well-constituted court for the trial of impeachments is an object not more to be desired than difficult to be obtained in a government wholly elective." Hamilton predicted correctly that an accusation leading to impeachment and trial would "agitate the passions of the whole community." Therefore, a process for accusing and trying public officials had to be carefully designed. And it was.

Impeachment is a method for defining and enforcing limits on executive and judicial behavior, essentially ensuring that no one is above the law. The Founders' use of this concept was derivative of English law. Ultimately, both the substance and process of impeachment replicated that of English practice. The terms "Treason, Bribery, or High Crimes and Misdemeanors" (Art. II, Sec. 4) were those used in English law. "Treason," and "Bribery" were obvious enough as deserving of impeachment; "High Crimes and Misdemeanors" were less certain, yet more likely to be used as a basis for bringing charges. Accordingly, intense debate was likely in those rare circumstances when a president was the subject (two occasions only: Andrew Johnson in 1868 and Bill Clinton in 1998, although Richard Nixon was threatened with impeachment in 1974, prior to his resignation motivated by the Watergate scandal).

The functions—impeachment and trial—were divided between the popularly elected House of Representatives, which was given the job of actual impeachment or indictment, and the elite-chosen Senate (by state legislatures prior to the ratification of the Seventeenth Amendment in 1913), which was responsible for the trial. This practice followed the English model of "the role of prosecutor to the [House of] Commons while the [House of] Lords sat in judgment."

But the Framers also were experienced with impeachment provisions in state constitutions. Those states providing for impeachment offered several methods for trials. So the Framers knew of options for managing the problem identified by Hamilton of removing an official who had been elected by the voters.

Reporting on August 6, the Committee of Detail opted for having impeachment tried before the Supreme Court, perhaps emulating the House of Lords, which served judicial functions in England. This proposal was controversial. Who would then try the justices if they were to be impeached? The issue was left for the Committee on Postponed Matters. As with the Electoral College, the committee settled on a masterful compromise. The Senate would try cases, with a two-thirds majority required for removal, and the Chief Justice of the United States would preside. The combination of the premier justice chairing the proceeding and a super majority required for removal might reduce partisanship by encouraging a more deliberative process (as was the case with Clinton).

The removal provisions were linked in the minds of delegates to those of election, reelection, and length of service. The fears of the Anti-Federalists and others suspicious of a strong national government might have been realized absent a method for impeachment and removal. Including such means suited the checks and balances essential for a system of separated powers.

Allocating and defining powers

By definition, executive powers tend to be derivative. An objective is required for execution to occur. Laws cannot be enforced before they are enacted; standards are not set in the abstract but to effect an agreed-upon purpose. It was, then, perfectly logical for the Founders to work first on delineating the powers of Congress, then to specify "The executive power shall be vested in a President of the United States of America," and finally to outline the judicial power of the courts in Article III. The sequence—Article I–Congress; Article II–Presidency; Article III–Judiciary—follows the ordinary progression of governance from making a law to its implementation and review.

This same point explains why it was unnecessary to specify each executive power. It was enough, for example, to state in Article I, Section 8, that "The Congress shall have Power To lay and collect Taxes." That specification implied that the executive would implement what Congress directed to be done—for example, to collect the taxes designed by Congress from those persons or groups specified in the law. Most Americans know just how that works in the case of the income tax, as administered by an executive agency—the Internal Revenue Service.

However, there were executive functions too that had to be defined in the Constitution. Who would make vital appointments? Who would command the military? Who would make treaties and assume other foreign policy functions? What would be the legislative role performed by the president? Who would act in national or international emergencies? These were among the most important governance-related issues that arguably could have been assigned to Congress as well as the executive. It is useful to be reminded that the answers to these questions are now familiar. But in 1787, each had to be explored, debated, and settled within the context of an overarching principle of separationism and governing purpose of unification.

Appointments

Designating the authority to make appointments was bound to be contentious given the inevitable competition among institutions in a separated powers system. Should Congress have appointing authority as a check on the executive? Or was that prerogative necessary for an effective executive? And who should be eligible to receive an appointment? In particular, should members of Congress be able to serve simultaneously in the executive or judicial departments?

The Virginia Plan provided for the legislature to elect the executive, essentially creating a parliamentary or unitary system. It might then have been logical for the plan to allow legislators to serve as ministers in the executive branch (as, for example, with members of Parliament in the United Kingdom). But the Virginia Plan disallowed such appointments. Legislators were not only "ineligible to any office established by a particular State, or under the authority of the United States," but, as well, they were not eligible for a period after leaving Congress.

The "ineligibility" provision was debated extensively, with a consensus developing on not permitting simultaneous service but serious questions raised about denying appointments for a period after departing. As finally resolved, ineligibility during legislative service was approved, and there was no provision added to disallow legislators having left Congress from being appointed, as many have.

The issue of who makes appointments was critical to the creation of a separation of powers system. The status of each branch was at stake. The Virginia Plan proposed that the legislature create tribunals and appoint judges. This provision was refined early in the Convention by giving the Senate the authority to appoint judges. The August 6 report of the Committee of Detail distributed appointments as follows: The treasurer would be appointed by the Legislature, ambassadors and judges of the Supreme Court by the Senate, and "officers in all cases not otherwise provided for by the Constitution" by the president.

As it had on other issues, the Committee on Postponed Matters chose a more executive-oriented process, one not previously voted on in the Convention. The president was given the authority to nominate and, "with the advice and consent of the Senate," appoint "ambassadors, and other public Ministers, Judges of the Supreme Court, and all other Officers of the U[nited] S[tates], whose appointments are not otherwise herein provided for."

The recommended language was almost exactly that finally adopted. The president was also given authority to fill vacancies during the recess of the Senate, and Congress could by law invest appointment of inferior officers "to the President alone, in the Courts of Law, or the Heads of Departments" (Art. II, Sec. 2). In the end, the Committee on Postponed Matters once again favored a distribution of powers such as to maintain a balance among the three branches.

The military

Among the president's greatest powers was one to which the Constitutional Convention devoted relatively few words: "The President shall be Commander in Chief of the Army and Navy." Seemingly it was assumed the executive would manage the militia, as was the case in the states. The more critical issue, of course, was that of deciding which branch would commit the nation to war.

Astonishingly, the decision to declare war received relatively little attention in Philadelphia. As accepted as it was that the president should command the militia, so too was it generally acknowledged that Congress should have the power to declare war. The only question was whether it should be the prerogative of the Senate only, and whether Congress had the power "to make war" or "to declare war." Making war suggested management and command. The report of the Committee of Detail used the words "make war," but on a floor motion the words were changed to "declare war." As one delegate pointed out, making war might be understood as "conducting" war, which properly would be an executive function.

Concerning these momentous issues, the delegates may have wasted few words in settling on their choices, but apparently the principle of separation guided them. Each institution was intended to bear significant responsibility for the military— whether to go to war and how. It has been an issue of major debate in the contemporary period with the changes in war itself encouraging greater presidential action in determining both when and how to use the military, most notably during the post–World War II era.

Treaty making

Lacking an executive, under the Articles of Confederation foreign policy and treaty making had to be managed by the unitary legislature. It was inevitable, then, that the Convention would have to decide how to allocate these matters if it was to agree on a separated powers system. It was likewise predictable that strengthening the executive, as happened during the course of the proceedings, would include an enhanced foreign policy role for the president. After all, there was no single leader of a bicameral legislature; rather, there were separate leaders for each chamber. Even so, not until the final weeks of the Convention was treaty making shifted from the Senate to the president.

Not unexpectedly, the Committee on Postponed Matters once again strengthened the president's role by suggesting the following language: "The President by and with the advice and consent of the Senate, shall have power to make treaties....But no Treaty shall be made without the consent of two-thirds of the members present." As reported in James Madison's notes, the debate focused on three issues: adding the House of Representatives for its advice and consent, excepting "treaties of peace" from the two-thirds requirement, and allowing treaties by consent of majority vote in the Senate. The first and third amendments were rejected; the second was first accepted, then rejected upon reconsideration. And so the Constitution in final form acknowledged the president as head of state with the authority to make treaties with the advice and two-thirds consent of the Senate. Surely adding the House of Representatives for advice and consent would have delayed treaty making in periods when party control was split between the House and the White House, and perhaps the Senate as well.

In practice, this authority conveyed to the president the initiative in foreign relations and international status as leader of the nation. Yet it also counseled foreign leaders that major decisions in the United States government ordinarily involved two or more branches of government. Many provisions in the Constitution may be viewed as tutorials in how a divided powers system works in its processes of *separating to unify*. The treaty-making provision was one such.

The legislative role

Providing a legislative or law-making role for the president was the subject of considerable debate at the Convention. Much of the discussion focused on the authority of the president to veto legislation passed by the House and Senate. Debate concentrated on what form the veto should take and the votes needed in the House of Representatives and Senate to override a veto. A related issue was whether to have the judiciary involved in vetoing. The Virginia Plan proposed a "council of revision" composed of the executive and the judiciary to review legislation and issue a "negative" or veto. The proposal was offered on three occasions in Philadelphia but was rejected each time. How would you have voted on that—essentially reviewing the constitutionality of laws as passed rather than awaiting a case before the court? It is interesting to consider the influence of such a process on the substance of lawmaking.

The idea of the veto itself was widely accepted. Those favoring domination of the executive, like Alexander Hamilton, wanted an absolute veto, that is, no further legislative recourse. This position was soundly defeated. Hamilton was not having a good convention. The issue then was the margin required to override the president's veto, the effect of which would be to enact legislation into law over the objections of the president. The Committee of Detail set the margin at two-thirds of the full membership of each house in its August 6 report. A motion was approved to increase the margin to three-fourths only to be changed back to two-thirds during the final days of the Convention. The two-thirds majority has proven to be a significant hurdle; only a very small proportion of vetoed measures become law as a result of overrides.

Less controversial lawmaking powers were, in time, to become vitally important in strengthening the legislative role of the president. Three interrelated clauses in particular are vital.

- "He may require the Opinion, in writing, of the principal Officers in each of the executive Departments, upon any Subject relating to the Duties of their respective Offices." (Art. II, Sec. 2)
- "He shall from time to time give to the Congress Information of the State of the Union." (Art. II, Sec. 3)
- "[He shall] recommend to their Consideration such Measures as he shall judge necessary and expedient." (Art. II, Sec. 3)

These three clauses provide the constitutional authority for an activist president to designate the agenda for Congress. The first invites the president to draw on the "Officers" of the departments in framing proposals. The third authorizes shaping this information and proposals into recommendations to Congress. And the second provides a formal provision of information on the State of the Union to Congress. And that is how it has worked in practice as "time to time" has come to be an annual stocktaking and agenda-setting message from the president to Congress. Indeed, with the coming of television, the message is one of those "national moments" that projects where we are as a people, expressed by the president, his supporters, and his critics at the Capitol and in the media.

Finally, the president is charged with taking "Care that the Laws be faithfully executed" (Art. II, Sec. 3). This "catchall" language was introduced in the report of the Committee of Detail on August 6 and carried through to the final report of the Committee of Style on September 12. It was, perhaps, the best that could be done in defining the intentions of executive powers but remains vague as to precise meaning or application. Still, presidents rely on this provision to validate an action that, arguably, cannot be justified by expressed authority in the Constitution or by existing statutes. Any use of this provision by presidents has, through history, been controversial. For that which lacks precise meaning is open to varying, and often partisan, interpretations when applied to issues of major importance.

Strengthening the executive

Inventors are problem solvers. Typically they tinker until they believe they have a workable device. It is often the case that inventors do not know in advance how well or how long their creations will work. The Founders were serious stylists as they worked at creating an executive branch. In so doing, they formed a government of separated powers. They had theories to guide them in their quest but very little practice with this form on a national scale. What emerged was a new experiment in democratic governance.

The executive progressed from weakness to strength in its shares of powers and competitive status in the government. The earliest decisions would have produced a congressional government, with the executive chosen by Congress and denied certain critical powers of appointment and treaty making. The later decisions provided an executive branch strong enough to hold its own against the other branches, without necessarily being able regularly to trump its competitors.

A strengthened executive contributed to fashioning a separated rather than unitary system of government. Governing powers in the Articles of Confederation were concentrated in Congress. Creating an executive who was independently elected and who had shares of governing authority produced a new and untried form of government—the separation of powers.

Table 1.1 Presidential Powers—Congressional Sharing (Required by US Constitution)

Presidential Powers	Congressional Sharing
Veto power (Art. I, Sec. 7)	Override by 2/3 of both houses (Art. I, Sec. 7)
Election (Art. II, Sec. 1; 12th Amendment)	Set the time; House chooses president, Senate chooses vice president if no majority in Electoral College (Art. II, Sec. 1; 12th Amendment)
Commander in chief (Art. II, Sec. 2)	"To declare War...To raise and support Armies...To provide and maintain a Navy" and other powers (Art. I, Sec. 8)
Make treaties (Art. II, Sec. 2)	Advice and 2/3 consent of Senate (Art. II, Sec. 2)
Selected appointments (including ambassadors, public ministers, and judges of the Supreme Court (Art. II, Sec. 2)	Advice and consent of Senate; vest appointment of inferior officers in others (Art. II, Sec. 2)
Give Congress information on the State of the Union and recommend measures (Art. II, Sec. 3)	"To make all Laws" (Art. I, Sec. 7) "No money...drawn...but in Consequence of Appropriations made in Law" (Art. I, Sec. 9)
Nominate a vice president in case of a vacancy (25th Amendment)	Majority vote in both houses (25th Amendment)
Removal (Art. II, Sec. 4)	House has sole power of impeachment; Senate has sole power of trying impeachments (Art. I, Secs. 2, 3)

Separated institutions sharing powers work within the constraints implicit in their having to share. As any sibling knows, it may be polite, even sociable, to share but it does leave less for you. Sharing can provoke competition so as to get as big a portion as possible. The Founders were ever sensitive to this tendency and worked to provide constraints, often literally forcing cross-institutional consultation and cooperation. Therefore, even a strengthened executive was constrained by checks and balances.

Effective governance in a separated system requires each branch to be attentive to the others. This principle appeared to dominate the thinking of the Founders. As applied to the presidency, it offers a rationale for a crucial theme: Presidents are not and cannot be as powerful as most people think. What was invented was an executive much stronger than any then existing in America, but one whose strength and effectiveness could only be realized in concert with the other branches. That is the essence of *separating to unify.* At no point in the creation was there any substantial opinion that in inventing the presidency the Founders were establishing *presidential government.* They wanted effective government, one in which the president would lead by being attentive to the legitimate roles played by the other branches.

Creating and strengthening the presidency ensured the emergence of a separation of powers. But doing so did not move the United States from a congressional to a presidential system. The lesson is clear: Understanding the presidency requires attention to its place in the government of separated institutions sharing and competing for powers. Presidential success or failure is often measured by the extent to which this lesson is absorbed and applied by the person who occupies the Oval Office.

Chapter 2
The presidency finds its place

Placing the presidency in the new government required answers to two questions of physical location: What city would serve as the capital? Where would the president live and work? Additionally, there was a question of enduring political interest: How would this recently invented executive work with the other branches?

As it happened, the same separationist rationale that evolved during the deliberations of the Constitutional Convention appeared to inform the responses to all three questions. The capital city would be sited in a central location, virtually at a midpoint between North and South. Congress and the presidency would be located in the city at some distance from each other, with a swamp separating the two buildings. And, save for failing to get a majority in the Electoral College, presidential candidates did not have to go through Congress to win. The two branches were to be independently elected, if interdependently empowered.

Today's visitors to Washington, DC, may find it difficult to believe but there was no such city when George Washington was inaugurated as the first president. Washington took the oath of office on April 30, 1789, on the balcony of Federal Hall, located at the corner of Wall and Broad Streets in New York City. New York, however, would not remain the executive's home for long.

An early debate sought to establish a permanent seat of government. Several locations were proposed as members of Congress favored their own states or regions. As finally resolved in July 1790, a Residency Act set the site for the capital on the Potomac River and authorized President Washington to appoint commissioners to designate its exact location. Meanwhile the government would stay in New York City until December 1790, then move to Philadelphia until 1800, after which a new, centrally located Federal City was expected to serve as the nation's capital.

With the first question of placement answered, the next uncertainties were the capital's precise location on the Potomac River and the design of the city. Land had been ceded by Maryland on the northeast side of the river, and by Virginia on the southwest side (unused, the latter section was later reclaimed by Virginia). President Washington selected the site, across the river from Alexandria, Virginia, not far from his home at Mount Vernon. He then appointed Major Pierre Charles L'Enfant, a French-born engineer who had served in the Continental Army, to plan a Federal City.

L'Enfant's design was not followed in every aspect, and Washington fired the temperamental planner along the way, but most people today would be able to identify L'Enfant's layout with its wide avenues, open blocks of space, and diagonals over an orderly grid as that of Washington, DC. Just as there was a desire at the Constitutional Convention to avoid centralizing power, the Federal City had no central location for government.

There were three governing centers in the new capital: one each for the Congress, the presidency, and the federal courts (the latter at Judiciary Square, though the Supreme Court was never located there). The executive and legislative branches were at the greatest distance, just over a mile apart, with the courts in between. This separation was likely to foster distinct communities, a development that occurred early and continued with the expansion of the

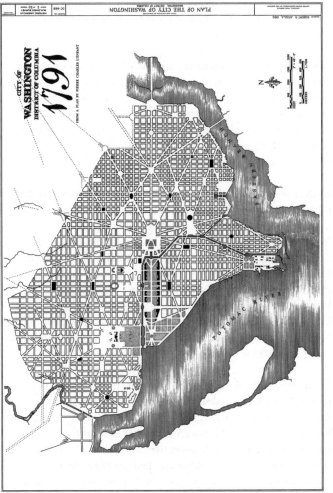

2. Major L'Enfant's design for the "Federal City," soon to be named for George Washington.

congressional and executive workforces. In fact, the distance between the branches allowed the communities to grow without impinging on one another, a condition that changed once the swamp between the Capitol and the executive mansion was drained.

What was originally called the President's House was designed as both residence and workplace. The building came to be referred to as the White House in the James Madison and James Monroe presidencies. How it got that name is a matter of some dispute. The most persuasive explanation is that it was rebuilt and painted white after being seriously damaged by a fire during the War of 1812.

So the answers to the first and second questions regarding real estate were that the presidency would be in a new city designated as the capital and would be housed in a building at some distance from Congress. In 1790 the city was named for the first president, a decision made by the three commissioners George Washington had appointed to assist him in deciding on the site for the new capital on the Potomac River. Interestingly, Washington never lived in the city bearing his name. He is the only president never to have lived in the White House, most assuredly to his relief as John Adams, its first resident president, found the building drafty, damp, and lacking a bathroom.

The answer to the third question regarding the place of the presidency in the government depended initially on the framework set forth in Article II, which concerned the executive branch. Three perspectives were evident at the Constitutional Convention in regard to the executive: a *presidential presidency* in which the executive would be the dominant branch; a *congressional presidency* with the executive selected by and thus dependent on Congress; and a *separated presidency* in which the executive and legislative branches shared and competed for powers as independently elected branches working interdependently.

Alexander Hamilton was the principal advocate of a presidential presidency. He proposed that the executive should be called "Governor" and be elected by electors "during good behavior," essentially a life term. The governor would have an absolute veto, full power as commander in chief, unrestricted appointing power for major departments, and the power to make treaties with the "advice and approbation" of the Senate.

There would have been little doubt about who was in charge had this plan been approved. Hamilton's plan received little or no support at the Convention and therefore did not represent an enduring perspective. The only immediate carryover was in the person of Hamilton, who was appointed secretary of the treasury in the Washington presidency, serving for more than five years and consistently supporting a strengthened executive.

Hamilton's perspective on the presidency may not have been styled by the Constitutional Convention but conditions have occasionally favored a strong executive. Because of crises, electoral support, incumbent's personality, and possibly all of these, some presidents (for example, Theodore Roosevelt, Woodrow Wilson, Franklin D. Roosevelt, Richard Nixon, and Barack Obama) view themselves as more Hamiltonian than Madisonian in their White House service. The term "imperial president" has often been applied to such cases.

The alleged polarization of American politics in the modern era, judged to produce gridlock, has seemingly encouraged presidents to rely more exclusively on executive power. Split-party control between Congress and the presidency contributes to this result, as displayed by the presidencies of George W. Bush and Barack Obama.

The congressional and separated presidency perspectives did not suffer the fate of Hamilton's plan in Philadelphia. The first had strong support at the Constitutional Convention among Anti-Federalists, ever wary of a powerful executive and a dominant central government. Indeed, congressional primacy characterized the set of proposals offered to the delegates by the Committee of Detail on August 6, 1787. Congress would choose the executive and have some executive-type functions (for example, treaty making by the Senate).

Most proposals along those lines were amended in the direction of a more independent executive, one not as strong as Hamilton's but with greater separation from Congress. Yet it was a certainty that those fearful of a too-strong executive would be ever watchful of how presidents interpreted and applied their authority. In fact, the balance of congressional versus presidential powers has been a focus of debate ever since 1787.

The final version of executive powers was that of the separated presidency, one independently elected and with shares of powers separate from those given to Congress. It was the most experimental of the three models and, therefore, the most subject to interpretation over time. Major events and personalities would likely influence the development of a presidency for which there was no analog, as would the need for the executive to work in concert with the other branches. Therein lay the boldness of the experiment, that is, in separating the institutions enough to prevent tyranny but not so much as to produce gridlock.

A congressional presidency?

What might have been? The Committee of Detail made several recommendations to the Constitutional Convention in regard to the executive branch on August 6, 1787. The proposals were in line with the original charter of the Convention, that is, to modify, not discard, the Articles of Confederation. Several proposals were also

Table 2.1 The Congressional Presidency That Might Have Been: Provisions Relating to the Executive in the Report of the Committee of Detail

Provision	Comment
Elected by the legislature	Seemingly the dominant view until the report of the Committee of Postponed Matters
Title to be "His Excellency"	Almost confirming the executive as ceremonial
Seven-year term	Many proposals, but seven-year term had the most support (was in the Virginia Plan)
Ineligible for a second term	A longer term justified ineligibility for reelection
Senate given power to make treaties and to appoint ambassadors and judges of the Supreme Court	Ordinarily thought of as executive powers; would have resulted in a weak executive
Legislature to appoint the treasurer	Another executive function given to the legislature
Members of Congress not eligible to serve in any other office; senators not eligible for one year after leaving office	Having the legislature elect the executive suggests a parliamentary system; making legislators ineligible to serve with the president interfered with development
Legislature given power "to make war"	Suggested Congress, not the commander in chief, would conduct war; later changed to "declare war"
Supreme Court to try impeachments	Changed later to the Senate when questions arose about trying judges

Source: Compiled by author from the report of the Committee of Detail as printed in Charles C. Tansill, *Documents Illustrative of the Union of the American States* (Washington, DC: US Government Printing Office, 1937), 471–82.

similar to those included in the Virginia Plan that served as the point of departure for the delegates.

A congressional presidency would have been created by the plan offered on August 6. There would not have been a separation of powers. Congress would select the president and the treasurer; the Senate would appoint ambassadors and judges of the Supreme Court. "His Excellency," the president, could serve but one seven-year term. The Senate-appointed Supreme Court would try impeachments. And Congress was to be given the power "to make war," the Senate "to make treaties."

Oddly, however, the report included a provision prohibiting members of Congress from serving in executive positions, with senators even banned from such jobs for a year after leaving the Senate. This proposal was at variance with parliamentary systems in which ministers are typically appointed from parliament. The delegates favoring this limitation were anxious to avoid cabals in which members of Congress would divide the spoils. But some delegates worried that the arrangement permitted presidents to select their friends and acquaintances for positions that would, over time, come to have significant powers without clear accountability to Congress, the body electing the executive in the first place.

As set forth in the Committee of Detail, Congress would circumscribe the president's place in the government. Once political parties developed and matured, their members in the legislature would select presidents and attempt to influence their appointments. Presidents would, in turn, be answerable to their party or a coalition of parties, much as in the United Kingdom. Presidents would not have an independent basis of support among voters apart from their public identity with the party. Even then, they would be limited to one seven-year term.

The Founders would have created a congressional presidency, marginally strengthening the executive provided for in the

Confederation but failing to invent an executive of sufficient independence to qualify as having met the criteria of a separated-powers government. Still this early plan revealed the hesitancy among many prominent delegates about having a strong, independent executive. Therefore, the first presidents were on notice to proceed cautiously in defining their status and exercising their powers.

A separated presidency

Through August 1787 and into September of that year, the Convention moved bit by bit toward an executive much less dependent on Congress. Creating an independently elected president with weighty powers over the executive branch was, perhaps, the most striking feature of the new government. However, the executive was not strengthened to the point of full self-determination, as Hamilton preferred. The veto could be overridden, treaties made required a two-thirds affirmative vote in the Senate, major appointments were with the advice and consent of the Senate, and the president as commander in chief needed support in Congress to go to war and to support and maintain the military.

The checks were real enough, but their purpose was not merely negative. The Founders were fashioning a mutually dependent lawmaking system. Each part of the system would support and enable the other two parts. The checks encouraged consultation both ways. In some cases, as with treaties and appointments, the Constitution even called for "advice" from the Senate. But politically savvy presidents would understand the need for communicating with those on Capitol Hill. If they wanted the legislation they inspired to be drafted and passed, they would need supporters from across the swamp on Capitol Hill. Likewise, if members of Congress wanted their causes supported by the president, they would need to be in his favor to avoid a veto. Political parties would facilitate this contact. Meanwhile, both the president and Congress would have to be ever wary of court

Table 2.2 Constitutional Provisions for the Separated Presidency: Powers and Checks

Powers	Checks in Congress
Veto bills	Reconsider and pass by 2/3 majorities in both houses
Fail to sign a bill	Becomes law within 10 days (Sundays excepted)
Fail to sign and Congress adjourns	No recourse
Commander in chief	To declare war, raise and support armies, provide and maintain a navy, regulate the land and naval force, call forth the militia, organize, arm, and discipline the militia
Require opinion of cabinet	No provision
Grant reprieves and pardons	No recourse
Make treaties	Advice and consent of 2/3 of senators present
Nominate and appoint ambassadors, other public ministers and consuls, and judges of the Supreme Court	Advice and consent of the Senate
Receive ambassadors	No provision
Fill vacancies during recess of Senate	No recourse
Give State of the Union message	No provision
Recommend measures to Congress	No provision (but require their approval to become law)
Convene both houses or either; adjourn them in case of disagreement	No recourse
Faithfully execute the laws	No provision
Nominate a vice president in case of a vacancy (25th Amendment)	Majority vote in both houses

judgments regarding the constitutionality of the agreements they reached.

Whether and how this concoction of shares of powers would work was uncertain on the launching of the revised government in 1789. Much would depend on events for testing the capacity of the interlocking system to manage. The sparseness of Article II on the executive provided few clues as to the president's role. Too much was left unwritten or unspecified. A great deal was left to be worked out over time, with incumbent presidents left to fill in the blanks.

Thus, for example, it would have been difficult at first to predict that obligations of the president to give Congress information on the State of the Union and to recommend measures for their consideration would serve vital agenda-setting functions. Nor would it have been apparent that the executive establishment would expand to immense proportions, thus challenging the management capabilities of the president and the oversight

3. President Barack Obama delivers the State of the Union message to a joint session of Congress—a feature of the separated presidency—in January 2013.

capacity of Congress. What the Founders may have foreseen was the variability in style, skill, adaptability, and savvy of individual presidents to fit themselves suitably into the job. And it was apparent that the distribution of powers and the ambiguities in defining these powers meant presidents would have to orient and reorient themselves to the power grids in Washington and outside. That these grids would eventually include thousands of private interests with lobbyists, a huge media component, non-governmental "think tanks," and representatives of foreign governments and international organizations was not at all obvious at the start.

The perpetual ordeal

If the Constitution and the government it created were to last, then it was inevitable that there would be two governing populations: those who came and went, and those who stayed on. Elected politicians and their aides mostly constitute the first group, a generalization modified in recent decades with high incumbency return on Capitol Hill. Judges with life appointments, bureaucrats, and contractors mostly comprise the second group. The first group would grow modestly as states were added; the second, especially the bureaucrats, professional staffs, and contractors would grow exponentially. Such developments are in the nature of a maturing government performing its functions in society.

Typically the expectations back home are that elected officials are in charge of the national government. The perpetual ordeal for those elected to serve for designated terms in Washington is to learn enough about the ways of those staying on to direct and oversee their work. The ordeal is especially apparent for presidents because more is expected of them, and they are among the shortest of short-termers.

George Washington's precedent of serving just two terms lasted for 152 years. During that span of time, nine of thirty-two presidents (including FDR) served a full eight years. One of these, Grover Cleveland, won two nonconsecutive terms (winning in 1884, losing in 1888, and winning again in 1892). Two others, Lincoln and McKinley, were elected twice but were assassinated.

Since the ratification in 1951 of the Twenty-second Amendment limiting a president to two terms, four of twelve presidents have served two full terms (Eisenhower, Reagan, Clinton, and George W. Bush), with Barack Obama in his second term at this writing. One, Nixon, was reelected but resigned.

What this record shows is that thirteen of forty-four presidents (30 percent) have served eight years (with one pending and one, FDR, having served twelve years). Eight years of service is equal to one and one-third Senate terms or four House terms. Yet most presidents do not serve that long. The average length of service of post–World War II presidents (excluding Obama) is 5.8 years—*not even one full Senate term.*

Presidents enter a permanent government for which they will be held responsible. The task was demanding enough at the start in 1789. It has come to be colossal with the expansion in the size and reach of the federal government. The challenge is especially daunting for someone who has not had direct governmental experience in Washington, a phenomenon that has occurred even in the modern period (four of six presidents, 1977–2016, having come from out of town, and Obama having been elected as a first-term senator).

The trial for George Washington as the first president was unique. "When Washington took the oath of office on April 30, 1789, he entered upon an office the nature of which was described only by certain sentences in an untried Constitution." It was not foreordained he would succeed. He was aided by his appointments.

Two future presidents served with Washington: John Adams as vice president and Thomas Jefferson as secretary of state. Alexander Hamilton served as secretary of the treasury. Edmund Randolph, a major figure at the Constitutional Convention, was attorney general. It was a strong start in giving life to a fresh national charter.

Who served first was important because the presidency needed the legitimate definition Washington and Adams were likely to provide. Jefferson had a different view, one much less supportive of a strong national government and influential executive. From Jefferson's presidency forward into the twentieth century, individual presidents would vary in regard to their perceptions of the role of presidential leadership. Typically, events such as economic recessions, foreign wars, and, most notably, the Civil War were influential in determining which presidents would be the most active. These events helped to define presidential leadership and explained the high ratings given by historians to Andrew Jackson, Abraham Lincoln, Theodore and Franklin Roosevelt, Woodrow Wilson, Harry Truman, and Ronald Reagan, in addition to Washington.

It was not until the twentieth century that presidents received much help in getting placed in an expanding government. They made appointments but had little personal professional assistance in the White House. This changed dramatically in the post–World War II period. Presidents now have several hundred assistants in the White House Office and hundreds more in a number of agencies in the Executive Office of the President. These many aides and supporting units serve as liaison to the scores of executive, legislative, and judicial agencies, essentially the president's fingers into the government.

Fitting in

Taking on a new job typically requires more than reading the job description and being sensitive to the growth of the organization. There are more subtle considerations, notably the status of the position at the time of employment. What were the effects of decisions made by the person leaving the job? Were people pleased with the predecessor's performance? What are the expectations in regard to decisions and behavior? Presidential scholar Stephen Skowronek adds this intriguing question: "How do presidents go about the task of fashioning their places in history, and how amenable are these places to being fashioned according to presidential design?"

A candidate should think about the true nature and complexities of the job before seeking it. In fact, one of the most important questions to be answered in deciding to run is this: Why do I want to be president? The future performance of the incumbent is a large part of the calculation. Having won, a president-elect's attention naturally turns to styling arrangements that will suit the purposes of seeking the job. But an election does not wipe the slate clean. A structure already exists. And policies set in place by previous administrations and congresses serve a purpose. Government endures; leadership changes.

Illustrations of the challenges facing new presidents abound. Consider what it must have been like for Franklin Roosevelt to take over in the midst of the Great Depression. Awesome challenges faced him and the Congress. In that case, government organization was insufficient to cope with economic and social issues. New agencies had to be created to administer bold new and challenging programs. Several entering presidents have had wars or their aftermaths to manage—Truman, World War II; Eisenhower, the Korean War; Nixon, the Vietnam War; Barack Obama, the war on terrorism. Whatever else these presidents wanted to accomplish had to be designed alongside decisions regarding the wars they inherited.

Other presidents are inaugurated in periods of huge expansions in government services. Eisenhower, a president with a mostly military career, was responsible for managing the New Deal and

Fair Deal social programs of FDR and Truman. Nixon inherited the Great Society domestic programs of Lyndon Johnson, a collection of entitlements such as Medicare, Medicaid, federal aid to education, and food stamps, which Nixon mostly did not favor, at least as formed.

The state of the economy and federal debt also can influence a president's options on moving into the White House. Reagan's priorities were dictated by double-digit inflation, high unemployment, and high interest rates at the end of the Carter presidency. Reagan's tax cuts stimulated the economy, but he mostly failed in an effort to cut back spending. Therefore, he passed on deficits and public debt that would restrict the choices of his successors. Clinton had to act first on the economy because of a recession in 1991–92, having to delay other priorities. What was labeled the "Great Recession" in 2008 was even more striking as an agenda-altering event facing Obama on his inauguration.

Scandal, too, has had carryover effects for new presidents. Truman (cronyism), Nixon (Watergate), Reagan (Iran-Contra), and Clinton (fundraising and Lewinsky)— each affected the presidency and how the next occupant judged it necessary to act, mostly with promises to develop and enforce codes of ethics.

Finally, reforms are often instituted in one presidency to affect another. Once in place, reforms (for example, the War Powers Act, 1973, or the Congressional Budget and Impoundment Control Act, 1974) are seldom abandoned by subsequent presidents or congresses, even if they are ineffective. Rather they become a part of the institution and therefore must be incorporated into how a presidency is managed.

Passing through

Presidents pass through a history they did not make but can influence. What came before is theirs to manage, along with the events that occur during their tenure and while acting on their own agenda of issues. Judging how to fit in will likely be prompted by how a person comes to be president. Some, such as FDR, Johnson, and Reagan, won by huge margins that reflected public anxiety for change. Each of these presidents was expected to propose large-scale programmatic shifts. They were encouraged to be *assertive* in the early months of taking over the presidency. Taken together, their presidencies were among the most productive of major policy change in recent history—Roosevelt and Johnson being more expansionist of government, Reagan being more consolidative and contractive.

More often, new presidents are advised to be cautious leaders because it is difficult to read the public mood. They will have won by the barest majority or, perhaps, by a plurality, making it very difficult to interpret a policy message from the election results. Fitting in requires attention to weaknesses as much as to strengths. Winning by an average popular vote percentage of 47 percent, Kennedy, Nixon, Carter, Clinton, and George W. Bush all had to heed this advice. Some did not. Carter (proposing a sweeping energy program), Clinton (setting national health care as a priority), and George W. Bush (campaigning for major change in Social Security in his second term) pressed forward with limited political or public support to endorse large change, all with limited or no success. Obama won with a larger margin, but his striking changes in national health care were enacted by narrow partisan margins in Congress and remained contentions through his presidency.

Certain presidents are custodial. They assume office on the death of their predecessors. "Fitting in" for Truman and Johnson included their sensitivity to the legacies of two popular presidents, FDR and John F. Kennedy (JFK). An argument can be made as well to include George H. W. Bush as a custodian of the Reagan presidency. He was said by some to be serving Reagan's third term. In each case, the takeover president had to respect the former leader's legacy while attempting to fashion a presidency suited to his own preferences—no simple task. Truman and Johnson were successful enough to be elected in their own right; George H. W. Bush was not. Johnson could be said to have more than fulfilled Kennedy's ambitious agenda.

In other cases, presidents are expected to be restorative of the institution because of scandal in the previous administration. Eisenhower, Ford, Carter, and George W. Bush were faced with emphasizing ethics as a priority because of scandals with previous administrations. Of these, Ford had the greatest challenge given the scope of Watergate and the resignation of President Nixon. Among other limitations was Ford's having been appointed, not elected, as vice president, the only president never to have won a national election. Ford's pardon of Nixon soon after being sworn in was heavily criticized, and Democrats won large majorities in the 1974 congressional elections. Ford's experience gave new meaning to the "perpetual ordeal."

Meeting expectations

Presidents face the formidable task of judging how to serve. Expectations for their performance vary but are mostly high. At first, presidents had to exercise caution in interpreting their authority. If they had been too aggressive, reforms would likely have been enacted to limit their powers. Through history, presidents have had to adapt to the larger responsibilities associated with a growing population, land mass, and bureaucracy. How each president adjusts to change inevitably affects the nature of the job for each successor. Accordingly, constitutional authority, how those prerogatives are interpreted, the impact of events on governing and government, and the performance, even personal behavior, of one's predecessor combine to delineate the job description for and public acceptance of presidents.

Not all presidents are created equal in the advantages available to them in finding their place in the government. Some come to Washington with little experience in the national government. Others become president by circumstance, the death or, in one case so far, the resignation of the president with whom they are serving as vice president. Presidents in each of these cases have special issues in finding their places.

Chapter 3
Electing presidents (and other ways to occupy the Oval Office)

To invent is to do something differently. The Founders invented a new form of validating executive leadership. Their design not only set forth an untried election system but also shaped the paths to and established the boundaries of presidential power. Much would be expected of those bearing the title of president, but their elections provided very different political capital for fulfilling those anticipations. And some presidents, one-fourth of those in the twentieth century, were not elected to the office when they first entered it.

Would it work? No one knew for certain at the start and, in fact, apart from accepting that George Washington would be the first president, no one knew exactly what would happen next. What a story it is! The mystery of the workings of the Electoral College may have played a role in its preservation. Setting reformist fervor aside, one has to admire the brilliance of fashioning an interlocking system so uninviting to quick-fix alterations. Tinkering with any one part—changing term lengths, choosing electors, counting electoral votes, substituting popular election—is fraught with unanticipated consequences.

Try it. Pick a favorite change in how presidents are elected. Then conduct a realistic test of the effects of your change. Think comprehensively about the system. Constitutional construction and history are on the side of maintaining the unique method designed by the Founders.

The political astuteness of the original formulation did not prevent anomalies in elections following the virtual coronations of George Washington for two terms. Corrections rather than reforms had to be made. For example, in 1796, the first election following Washington's retirement, John Adams and Thomas Jefferson were logical choices as candidates. Adams was completing his second term as vice president; Jefferson was the principal author of the Declaration of Independence and the first secretary of state. Adams won narrowly. Having placed second, Jefferson served as Adams's vice president. In a contemporary context, it would be akin to John McCain, followed by Mitt Romney, Republican opponents in 2008 and 2012, serving as Barack Obama's vice presidents. It is hard to imagine that arrangement would work very well.

These same two candidates—Adams and Jefferson—ran in 1800, this time with the endorsements of congressional caucuses—Federalists for Adams, Democratic-Republicans for Jefferson. The result was a tie, not between Jefferson and Adams but between Jefferson and his running mate, Aaron Burr. That anomaly had to be corrected, and it was in the Twelfth Amendment.

Originally, the Constitution provided that state legislatures would design a method for appointing presidential electors in their jurisdiction. The number of electors allocated to a state was the total of its representatives and senators. The electors were to meet in each state and vote for two persons. Their tallies in each state were sent to the president of the Senate to be counted. The person receiving a majority of the votes would be president. Originally, if two persons received an equal majority, as with Jefferson and Burr in 1800, the House of Representatives would choose between them. Similarly, if no one person received a majority of electors, the House of Representatives would again choose, this time from among the top five vote-getters. In either case, the person receiving the second most electors would serve as vice president, with the Senate making the choice if two or more candidates had an equal number of votes.

This method of election was, to say the least, unusual, even bizarre. It disregarded the probability that political parties would develop. It allowed for the popular election of electors but did not require it. Thus, an aristocratic method of appointing electors was allowed, along with a democratic method of popular election. And the election of the vice president was a party-less matter; essentially, this office was held by whoever came in second, as with Jefferson serving as Adams's vice president in 1796.

How would the Electoral College system get under way? In the first election in 1789, the electors all voted for Washington. How they were appointed made no difference as there was no opponent. Still, the method varied among the states. Some state legislatures, in joint session or concurrently, appointed electors; others had a variation of popular election and designation by the state legislature. Three states did not participate in 1789: New York because the two houses of the state legislature could not agree on a method, and North Carolina and Rhode Island because they had not as yet ratified the Constitution. Washington received sixty-nine electoral votes. Electors had two votes, one each for president and vice president, and while there was no stated opposition to Washington, opinions varied regarding a second choice. John Adams had the most second-ballot votes, but fewer than Washington, and thus, coming in second, served as vice president.

The matter of first and second place was bound to cause problems at some point. What if two candidates received an equal number of votes? The Constitution provided that the contest would then go to the House of Representatives. But if that were to happen frequently, as some Founders thought it would, the principle of the separation of powers might be subverted by Congress effectively making the choice. Further, in such situations as Jefferson serving as vice president with Adams, one's opponent might then take over on the death or resignation of the president.

It did not take long for these issues to be dealt with. In 1800, Thomas Jefferson, at that time the vice president, was a candidate for president. Aaron Burr was running for vice president. Both received seventy-three electoral votes. The Constitution specified that electors "vote by Ballot for two persons," making no provision for separate balloting for president and vice president. Under these circumstances, the House of Representatives was directed to "chuse by Ballot one of them for President" (Art. II, Sec. 1). As president of the Senate, Jefferson himself announced the result: a tie.

As provided in Article II, voting in the House for this purpose was by states, with each state *having one vote* regardless of the number of its representatives. On the first ballot, Jefferson won eight states, Burr six, and the delegations from two states were divided and thus had no vote. Nine states were required for election. It took thirty-six ballots and a great deal of political dealing for Jefferson to get the ninth state. Imagine the chaos in governing had this method not been righted.

In 1803, Congress passed a constitutional amendment requiring electors "to vote by ballot for President and Vice President," thereby separating the two positions. This Twelfth Amendment was quickly ratified and was therefore in place for the 1804 election. The Electoral College method of selection has not been the subject of other constitutional amendments. The nominating and election processes have, however, evolved over time as quite different from those early contests.

An evolving system

The ambiguity illustrated by the 1800 election was but one of several issues to be resolved. Who would be the candidates?

Would there be political parties? Would presidential and vice presidential candidates run as a team? How would electors be chosen? Answers to these questions illustrate the complexities in proposing reforms. The system came to be interconnected, with political parties taking a strong interest in candidate selection given their stake in team victories.

Events leading to the creation of a United States of America were bound to produce likely candidates for president. There was an ample supply of notable figures actively involved in public affairs: John Adams, Thomas Jefferson, Alexander Hamilton, Aaron Burr, Thomas Pinckney, John Jay, James Madison, and George Clinton, to name a few. Benjamin Franklin too was an eminent figure, though elderly at the founding, and he died a year afterward. Too bad. A Franklin presidency would have enlivened government, politics, and social life. Consult any biography of the Philadelphian to understand why.

Congressional caucuses

Congressional caucuses—meetings of like-minded senators and representatives—developed as the means for nominating presidential candidates for several early elections. Their emergence was viewed by some as jeopardizing the separation of institutions that had been achieved at the Constitutional Convention. For if presidents had first to be nominated by members of Congress, would they not then be in the members' debt? As it was, however, the caucuses during this period, 1804–24, mostly selected expected, if not always certain, choices. Twice, in 1812 and 1820, the Democrat-Republicans nominated incumbent presidents, Madison and Monroe. The Federalists were declining steadily during this time and were no longer a factor by 1820.

The period between 1824 and 1832 proved to be critical for presidential nominations and the development of political parties. In 1824, the congressional caucus system became an issue. A small group of Democrat-Republicans caucused to nominate Secretary of the Treasury William Crawford for president. Other, regional candidates did not accept this choice and were nominated within their states rather than by the caucuses. As a consequence, the voters and electors were given four choices: Andrew Jackson of Tennessee; John Quincy Adams of Massachusetts (son of John Adams); William Crawford, the rump caucus nominee from Georgia; and Henry Clay of Kentucky.

Jackson won a plurality of the popular and electoral vote but did not have a majority of either. Therefore the choice fell to the House of Representatives, again voting by states but this time among the top three, Jackson, Adams, and Crawford, as provided by the Twelfth Amendment. Having come in fourth, Clay threw his support to Adams, who won the required majority of thirteen states on the first ballot. Jackson was understandably enraged. President Adams rewarded Clay by appointing him secretary of state. It is interesting that two of the most controversial elections in history, 1824 and 2000, involved the sons of former presidents: John Quincy Adams and George W. Bush.

National conventions

The brief era of the congressional caucus as a nominating body was over in 1824. The circumstances of its demise showed that a more popular method for selecting presidential candidates had to come into being. The 1824 election had made clear that the public did not support having members of Congress control who would be their choices for president. It also marked the end of the Founders' generation, and with it, the Federalists as a political force. Additionally, the failure of the Democrat-Republicans to unify behind one candidate caused their downfall.

In 1828, Andrew Jackson was renominated by the Tennessee legislature and became the consensus candidate of the new Democratic Party. Those supporting the reelection of President

John Quincy Adams called themselves the National Republicans. There was no disputing the results in 1828; Jackson won the Electoral College by a margin of more than 2 to 1 over Adams.

Some form of mass party meeting at this time was predictable if the presidential nomination was to come from outside Washington, DC. The first such conclave was held in September 1831 by the Anti-Masons, a third party. The National Republicans followed with a convention in December 1831, and they also prepared the first party platform; the Democrats held their first meeting in May 1832. This new form for nominations had staying power, if variable functions, over time. Every major party candidate from 1831 to the present has been formally nominated by a national convention.

It was also predictable that attention would eventually turn to the selection of delegates to the nominating conventions. Those wishing to have influence with or to be rewarded by a president sought first to control state delegations to national conventions. As political parties gained strength, state and local bosses bargained for appointments and policy with candidate organizations. Party bosses and presidential candidates regularly negotiated for support and payoffs in the nomination process.

On occasions, these negotiations carried through to the conventions, with disputes on seating the delegations, writing the platform, and choosing candidates. Prior to the development of presidential primaries, multiple ballots were often required to nominate presidential and vice presidential candidates, especially in the Democratic Party because of its two-thirds rule for winning the nomination. Thirteen of the twenty-four Democratic conventions from 1832 to 1924 required more than one ballot. Seven took more than ten ballots, four more than forty. The record was 103 ballots for the Democrats in 1924. The two-thirds rule was abandoned in 1936, and there has been just one multi-ballot Democratic convention since—the one in 1952.

Republican rules have always provided for a simple majority in nominating their candidates. They had eight multi-ballot conventions of the seventeen between the founding of the party in 1856 and 1920. Just one of these exceeded ten ballots: thirty-six were required in 1880. Subsequently, Republicans have made their nominations with one ballot in all but two conventions, 1940 and 1948. Having lost the drama of choosing the candidate, conventions are of less interest to the public while retaining other purposes, notably for unifying the party in kicking off the general election campaign.

Presidential primaries

The development and refinement of presidential primaries are major reasons for the one-ballot convention in the modern period. In 1901 Florida was the first state to provide a primary election for choosing delegates to the national convention. Wisconsin followed in 1905, Pennsylvania in 1906, and Oregon in 1910. By the 1912 conventions, a dozen states had adopted some form of the primary (either for the selection of delegates or for permitting voters to express preferences among candidates, or both); another eight had done so by 1916. But enthusiasm for primaries began to wane in the 1920s and '30s. Several states repealed their laws. Most party leaders were not keen about primaries given that they were substituting voter choice for local and state leader control of delegations. During the 1930s, public attention was focused on the Depression and World War II, with President Roosevelt dominating national politics. There were twenty primaries in 1920 and just fourteen in 1940, almost none of which was seriously contested in either party.

Presidential primaries were revived following World War II as a popular route to the nomination. Those candidates not favored by party leaders could win if they were able to garner sufficient delegate support. The greater ease of travel and communication enabled prospective candidates to manage national campaigns and potentially to establish front-runner status prior to the convention.

Primaries were important in both the Democratic and Republican nomination battles in 1952. Senator Estes Kefauver (Tennessee) challenged Democratic Party leaders by running in primaries. He won twelve of the fifteen in 1952 and forced a three-ballot convention, won by Illinois Governor Adlai Stevenson, who received less than 2 percent of the primary vote. In the Republican Party, General Dwight D. Eisenhower successfully challenged the establishment candidacy of Senator Robert A. Taft (Ohio). Eisenhower won five of the nine contests in which he was entered, bolstered by his World War II leadership in Europe and his above-politics favorability, embodied in his "I Like Ike" campaign slogan.

From 1952 forward, candidates were expected to establish front-runner status by winning primaries even though a majority of delegates were selected by other means, mostly state party caucuses. The number of primaries increased only slightly between 1952 and 1964, varying between fifteen and nineteen. But in each case the candidate with the most primary votes won the nomination.

The 1968 Democratic nomination proved to be vital in solidifying the role of primaries. President Lyndon Johnson decided not to seek reelection, thus providing an open race for the nomination. The principal candidates were Senators Eugene McCarthy (Minnesota) and Robert Kennedy (New York). McCarthy won the early primaries before Kennedy entered the race. Kennedy won the critical California primary but was assassinated on the very evening of his victory. Vice President Hubert Humphrey did not enter the primaries, receiving only write-in votes. The principal issue was the Vietnam War, with McCarthy and Kennedy opposed and Humphrey representing the Johnson administration's record in directing the war.

The 1968 Democratic convention was among the most tumultuous in history. Humphrey was the choice of party leaders, but he had not been tested in the primaries. Kennedy, the emerging popular choice, was dead. Antiwar activists were desperate. Riots broke out in Chicago, the convention city, as Humphrey won the nomination. Post-convention reform commissions concentrated on ensuring a more open process with greater representation of all groups. These changes made by the reform commissions encouraged many more states to adopt presidential primaries. The number of primary states increased from the mid-twenties in 1976 to the mid-thirties in the 1980s, the high thirties in the 1990s, and more than forty at the millennium.

By the end of the century, nominations were settled in presidential primaries, with the front runner in each party selected by the convention in every case from 1972 to 2012. Conventions became ratifying agencies of a choice already made. Additionally, states began front-loading their primaries; that is, moving them earlier in the calendar. Consequently, the campaign for the nomination started earlier, front runners emerged from the first primaries, and the general election campaign began months sooner than in the past. Understandably, these developments have added to the cost of running for president and have resulted in renewed demands for campaign finance reform even as fundraising has eased into the billions of dollars.

Presidential primaries are great political theater for television coverage. Dramatic developments in communication have had a profound effect on the nominating process. Like horse races, campaigns are interesting to follow. They take place in the open, the stakes are high, and they have a finish line—election day. But television, the Internet, and other forms of electronic and wireless communication are also incorporated into individual campaigns, at an increasingly high cost in dollars and organizational effort.

The nomination of presidential candidates has thus evolved historically in several stages: expected choice of national figures, congressional caucus endorsement, national party conventions, conventions supplemented by primaries, primaries establishing front runners, and primaries determining the choice among candidates. These stages reflect intentions to have the public involved, basically responding to more general democratizing developments, such as the emergence of political parties, expansion of suffrage, state electoral reforms, and stunning advances in mass media and campaign technology.

Political parties: winning elections

In *Federalist No. 10*, James Madison warned against "the mischiefs of faction," stressing the need to control their effects. Madison defined faction as "a majority or minority of the whole, who are united or actuated by some common impulse of passion, or of interest, adverse to the rights of other citizens, or to the permanent and aggregate interests of the community." He believed the Founders had discovered the formula for regulating faction: representative government extended over "a greater variety of parties and interests." Put simply: Make a republic and extend its sphere.

In *Federalist No. 51*, Madison justified the separation of powers and checks and balances by a similar acknowledgment of the need for controls. "Ambition must be made to counterattack ambition.... A dependence on the people is, no doubt, the primary control on the government; but experience has taught mankind the necessity of auxiliary precautions." Thus it was that the Founders made it virtually impossible for a faction, whether as a political party or an interest group, to direct the whole divided government.

The constitutional design did not, however, prohibit either faction or party. Madison explained that removing the causes of common impulses or interests would be wrong or impractical. A free society

Table 3.1 Major Political Parties in Competition for the Presidency, 1789–2016

Period	Political Party A	Political Party B
1789–96	Federalist	—
1800–16	Federalist	Democratic-Republican
1820–24	Independent Democratic-Republican	Democratic-Republican
1828–32	National Republican	Democratic-Republican
1836–52	Whig	Democrat
1856–2016	Republican	Democrat

Source: Compiled by author from Harold W. Stanley and Richard G. Niemi, *Vital Statistics on American Politics*, 3rd ed. (Washington, DC: Congressional Quarterly Press, 1992), 111–15.

thrives on the right to organize in support of common interests. And so it was a matter of when and how political parties would develop, not whether. From 1856 to the present, the competition has primarily been Democrats versus the Republicans. Minor parties have been a factor along the way, but none since 1856 has achieved lasting national competitive status.

How have political parties advanced? And what difference has their progress made for presidential elections? Importantly, Madison and his colleagues designed an elaborate set of effective boundaries. Federalism, separation of powers, separation of elections, checks and balances, bicameralism, variable and staggered term lengths, and the Electoral College have determined how political parties function. The design did not prevent parties or factions from emerging, but it created the box within which they would do their work.

This constitutional structure has nurtured political parties as loose, election-based, mostly nonideological, interest-promoting-and-facilitating organizations of a self-identifying membership.

Third parties with more programmatic and ideological orientations have not prospered for long. True, the Republican Party tends to be more conservative, less likely to promote government solutions, and more representative of business interests. The Democratic Party tends to be more liberal, more likely to favor a larger role for government, and more representative of labor's interests. But both tents are large, and regional differences have been substantial, if shifting in recent decades.

It has been said that banks are robbed because that is where the money is. Likewise, political parties organize where the elections are. And by constitutional intention and allowance, elections are everywhere. Most relevant for presidents are those contests for their job and those for the House of Representatives and Senate. In many respects these are all state elections, subject as they are to regulations at that level. Accordingly, political parties adjust to state laws regulating how they organize, select candidates, manage elections, and raise and spend money.

Term lengths have an effect on how political parties organize and function. If presidents, representatives, and senators all had coterminous four-year terms, the political party could conceivably coordinate the campaign messages and fashion leadership strategies for governing. But a president is elected with representatives who are then up for reelection in two years and with just a third of the senators whose terms will not end for six years, two years beyond that of presidents unless the presidents are reelected.

The Founders separated the powers by separating the elections. That fact is basic for understanding the workings of American politics. In sharp contrast with a parliamentary system, American political parties organize to win the three institutions: the House, a third of the Senate, and the presidency. Each party has campaign committees in the House and Senate to raise money and coordinate election activities. Presidential candidates have their own campaign committees, and the national party committees attempt to harmonize these units. This separation within the party structure is shaped by the differences among the three types of national elections (president, House, partial Senate). The campaigns for each vary in fundraising, agenda, the stakes (different term lengths), applicable laws, types of candidates, and connections to state and local parties. The problems of coordinating all of these organizations are avoided, in a sense, by not having anyone in charge.

One clear and wholly constitutional effect of separating national elections is to allow both political parties to win. For example, in 1996 President Clinton, a Democrat, was handily reelected president and Republicans kept their House and Senate majorities. Such split-party results make it difficult to declare a mandate. Seemingly, voters often accept the advice of baseball's Yogi Berra: "When you come to the fork in the road, take it!"

There are six combinations of split results with two parties and three elections. All six variations have been realized from the founding of the current two-party system in 1856. Split-party results were common in the second half of the nineteenth century, occurring nearly 50 percent of the time. It was rare during the first half of the twentieth century to have one party in the White House, the other a majority in Congress. In the post–World War II era, however, split-party government has been the common form. Nine of the twelve presidents in that time have at some point faced opposite party majorities in one or both houses of Congress. Remarkably, the parties split control of the presidency and Congress for one twelve-year period, 1981–93. Furthermore, the two branches had split control for nearly 80 percent of the time, 1969–2017. Seven of eight presidents during this forty-eight-year period had to work at some point with congressional majorities of the opposite political party.

Table 3.2 Forms of Split-Party Arrangements, 1856–2016

Presidency	House	Senate	Examples
Democrat	Republican	Republican	Cleveland, 1895–97; Wilson, 1919–21; Truman, 1947–49; Clinton, 1995–2001; Obama, 2015–17 = 14 years.
Democrat	Republican	Democrat	Buchanan, 1859–61; Obama, 2011–15 = 6 years.
Democrat	Democrat	Republican	Cleveland, 1885–89 = 4 years.
Republican	Democrat	Democrat	Hayes, 1879–81; Eisenhower, 1955–61; Nixon-Ford, 1969–77; Reagan, 1987–89; GWHBush, 1989–93; GWBush, 2007–09 = 24 years.
Republican	Republican	Democrat	Garfield, 1881–83; GWBush, 2001–03 = 4 years.
Republican	Democrat	Republican	Grant, 1875–77; Hayes, 1877–79; Arthur, 1883–85; Harrison, 1891–93; Taft, 1911–13; Hoover, 1931–33; Reagan, 1981–87 = 18 years.

Source: Compiled from data in Norman J. Ornstein et al., *Vital Statistics on Congress, 2001-2002* (Washington, DC: AEI Press, 2002), 56–58.

The consequences for political parties of separating elections and staggering terms of office are profound. The party a president defeated in winning office may command House and/or Senate majorities. In that case, presidents must seek cross-party support in enacting a program. Presidents with opposition party congresses also may find that too much compromising with the other side loses votes in their own party. Sometimes you cannot even win by winning.

Presidents obviously prefer that their party has majority status in the House and Senate. That advantage, however, does not guarantee loyalty. The staggering of terms (two, four, and six years) means all representatives and one-third of senators will face election in two years. The strong incentive on Capitol Hill is to bring constituency-oriented perspectives to presidential requests. State and local interests often trump party loyalty.

Continuous testing

Presidential and congressional elections occur by the calendar, not in reaction to crises, votes of confidence, or even deaths. Thus, it is entirely possible to have an election with relatively few issues; the contest in 1988 was said by analysts to be one such. By law, presidential and congressional elections occur on the first Tuesday after the first Monday in November. Having a designated day structures the campaign, in terms of organization, candidate activity, and expenditure of funds. Among other important dates on the calendar are those for candidate announcement, presidential caucuses and primaries, the two national conventions, and candidate debates.

Candidates and parties take polls continuously, and these polls often dominate media coverage of the campaign. In the period after World War II, there was only one major polling organization—the Gallup Poll. Today there are many. Most major media outlets—national newspapers and magazines, network and cable television—sponsor polls, with state and local polls arranged by media at those levels. Universities and institutes, candidate organizations, and political parties also conduct surveys and polls. These measures of opinion largely concentrate on the candidates. Who is ahead and by how much? Tests are taken on issues as well and may influence campaign rhetoric and debate. Election day ordinarily settles who will be president. An exception was the 2000 election, when a recount in Florida delayed the final outcome until mid-December. Until recently, campaigning ceased on election day, and the organizational stages of governing by a new team began. The political consultants moved on to other clients, and the pollsters conducted fewer tests. All of that has changed dramatically, with the lines less clearly drawn.

Permanent campaigning is now a notable feature of governing. Polls are regularly taken on major issues, and the president's job approval is tested frequently. In his first three years in office, President George W. Bush had a total of 630 ratings of his job performance; 210 a year, nearly eighteen a month. He was evaluated as many times in a week as President Truman was in a year. President Barack Obama's performance is subject to daily tests by two polling organizations, with averages of dozens of current polls calculated every twenty-four hours.

What explains this exponential growth in testing the public's view of how well the president is doing the job? Improvement in the technology of polling is part of the answer. Now it is easier than in the past to produce, analyze, and report poll results. Why are the results of interest? After all, the president is in office for a fixed, four-year term. Split-party government, a more open policy process, and, more recently, narrow-margin politics between the political parties help to explain why more polls are taken and the results heeded. Each cause merits comment.

The need for presidents to work with an opposite party majority on Capitol Hill generates interest in their political status in both parties. High job-approval ratings are thought to be evidence of public support, at least at the time of the poll, and are therefore a potential advantage for the president in building congressional majorities. Members of Congress, especially those from states or districts won by the president, are understandably attentive to these scores.

Related to this result is a tendency for policy debates to be more in the public domain, typically facilitated by mass media coverage. Virtually all major legislation is now the subject of advertising on television, heated discussion on talk radio and cable news stations, analysis by Internet bloggers, and sometimes mass demonstrations. Hence there are policy horse races just as there are candidate horse races. It is thought that one way to judge who is winning is to take polls.

Narrow-margin politics have advanced these developments. The 2004 presidential election was the first since 1988 in which the winner garnered a majority of the popular vote, but by just 51 percent. House and Senate majorities have been thin for more than twenty years (1995–2017), thus placing a premium on party unity—the closer the margin, the greater is the value of each vote. Again, the president's political status as measured by public support is a factor in effective leadership of a narrowly divided Congress.

These trends in polling, policy, and politics encourage presidents to campaign actively and constantly. Contemporary presidents campaign for policy directly with the public. It is now common for presidents to take to the road following the announcement of a major proposal. Thus the effectiveness of contemporary presidents is checked constantly, even daily. They make an effort to influence those ratings so as to maintain imposing political status.

Who wins?

From 1856 to 2016 there have been forty elections and twenty-six elected presidents (not counting Andrew Johnson, Chester Arthur, and Gerald Ford, who served but were never elected as president). Republicans have won a majority of the elections in the period. Democrats dominated the presidency during just one period, 1932–52, when Franklin D. Roosevelt won four times and Truman once. Republicans won 74 percent of the elections from 1856 to 1928 and 56 percent of those from 1952 to 2016.

Table 3.3 Winning the Presidency, 1856–2016 (40 elections)

Feature	Democrats	Republicans
Elected and reelected	17 (43%)	23 (57%)
Number of persons	10 (38%)	16 (62%)
Reelected	4 (FDR 3 times)	7
Elected twice nonsequentially	1 (Cleveland)	0
Defeated for reelection	2 (Cleveland, Carter)	4 (B. Harrison, Taft, Hoover, GHWBush)
VPs succeeding	2 (Truman, L. Johnson)	5 (A. Johnson, Arthur, T. Roosevelt, Coolidge, Ford)
Successors elected to full terms	2 (Truman, L. Johnson)	2 (T. Roosevelt, Coolidge)
Successor defeated for full term	0	1 (Ford)

Source: Compiled by the author, primarily from data in Michael Nelson, ed., *Guide to the Presidency,* 2nd ed. (Washington, DC: Congressional Quarterly Press, 1996), 1667–69. Post-1996 data collected from Internet sources.

Just four Democrats (Wilson, FDR, Clinton, and Obama) were reelected from 1856 to 2016 (FDR three times), although Cleveland served two nonconsecutive terms. Seven Republicans were reelected (Lincoln, Grant, McKinley, Eisenhower, Nixon, Reagan, and George W. Bush). Of those reelected, Lincoln, McKinley, FDR, and Nixon did not complete their terms (in FDR's case, his fourth). Two Democratic presidents were defeated for reelection (one, Cleveland, was subsequently elected to a second term), as were four Republicans.

How one is elected may differ significantly from one presidential election to another, and that variation can have a profound effect on a president's political influence in Washington. In many

Table 3.4 Close Presidential Elections, 1856–2016

Results	Democrats (year)	Republicans (year)
Popular Vote		
Won by plurality (12)	9: Buchanan (1856), Cleveland (1884, 1892), Wilson (1912, 1916), Truman (1948), Kennedy (1960), Clinton (1992, 1996)	3: Lincoln (1860), Garfield (1880), Nixon (1968)
Won by 50–52% (7)	2: Carter (1976) Obama (2012)	5: McKinley (1896, 1900), Taft (1908), Reagan (1980), GWBush (2004)
Lost (3)	0	3: Hayes (1876), B. Harrison (1888), GWBush (2000)
Electoral Vote		
Won by 50–55% (7)	3: Cleveland (1884), Wilson (1916), Carter (1976)	4: Hayes (1876), McKinley (1900), GWBush (2000, 2004)

Source: Compiled from data in Harold W. Stanley and Richard G. Niemi, *Vital Statistics on American Politics*, 3rd ed. (Washington, DC: Congressional Quarterly Press, 1992), 113–15, and Internet sources for recent elections.

elections since 1856, the winner lacked a decisive victory in the popular or electoral vote or both. Several points are notable:

- More than half of the elections (twenty-two of forty) were narrowly won.

- The number of close elections is equally divided between the parties: eleven Democrats, eleven Republicans.

- Two-thirds of the presidents in close elections (fifteen of twenty-two) did not receive a majority of the popular vote, including three who lost it (Hayes, Harrison, and Bush 43).

4. Inauguration: A national ceremony and public celebration for the new or reelected president.

- In one-third of the elections (seven of twenty-two), the winners had slim approval in both the popular and electoral counts.
- More than two-thirds of these twenty-two presidencies with close elections also faced opposition party control of one or both houses of Congress at some point in their terms. Additionally, seven of the presidencies with comfortable wins also faced opposition party control on Capitol Hill.

These numbers are profoundly important for understanding the political status and policy challenges of a presidency in the separated system. Presidents enter and reenter the White House with variable public endorsements as measured by the special combination of popular and electoral vote, supplemented by the independent results of congressional elections. Victory for many presidents authorizes a location for exercising power—the White House—but little else by way of political capital at the start. Legitimate occupancy of the office is, unquestionably, an affirmation of position and institutional status. But it is notable that more than half of the presidents, from 1856 to 2016, have had to strengthen their standing virtually from their inauguration forward. Their motivation for doing so is clear enough given that they are held accountable for governing whether or not they have the political resources to rule. The bottom line goes something like this: Being elected president is but the first step in the exercise of power.

Becoming president by other means

Seven vice presidents have succeeded the president with whom they served. Death was the reason in six cases, resignation in one (Nixon). This total represents 16 percent of all presidents. Five of the seven sought election to a full term, four winning (Truman and Lyndon Johnson among Democrats, Theodore Roosevelt and Coolidge among Republicans) and one losing narrowly (Ford). Succeeding vice presidents have served just over thirty-five years, twenty-eight of those years coming since 1901.

It is true that vice presidents are elected along with presidents, but their selection is typically more akin to an appointment. Presidential nominees choose their running mates, most often based on their assessment of how their choice will aid the campaign and contribute to their presidency if they win. Vice presidents cannot ordinarily predict whether or when they will move into the Oval Office. Therefore they cannot plan to do so in any serious way. They profit from proximity and from performing whatever tasks presidents assign to them. Recent presidents, at least from Carter to Obama, have given their vice presidents serious responsibilities. During this time (1977–2016), three ran for president—Mondale in 1984, George H. W. Bush in 1988, and Gore in 2000. Only Bush was elected.

Proximity and weighty assignments familiarize vice presidents with the issues and processes of presidential leadership. When the unexpected happens and vice presidents take the oath of office, they assume leadership of a presidency created and shaped for someone else. Typically it is not possible in the short run to reconstitute the office, cabinet, and other major posts to suit the style and goals of the new president. It is not workable to have wholesale turnover. Why? Because the successor needs staff and agency heads to help with the transition, talented and experienced staff are not immediately available as replacements, and precipitate change will likely be interpreted as a rejection of the departed president. These issues were not as important in earlier times when staffs were small and appointments few. But they are vital in contemporary times. Consequently, successors may have to wait until they win a full term before reshaping their predecessor's presidency to suit their policy agenda and style of serving. Four twentieth-century successors have had that opportunity— Theodore Roosevelt, Coolidge, Truman, and Lyndon Johnson.

No two alike

The Founders designed a unique election system, one so special that exactly how it would work was uncertain. Presidents were to be elected for four-year terms by electors, not directly by the people. Representatives were to be elected for two-year terms by the people and senators for six-year terms by state legislatures (changed much later to popular election by the Seventeenth Amendment). This modified democratic arrangement has shaped much of national politics, specifying as it does the opportunities and constraints that define presidential power. History abounds with efforts to further democratize how presidents and members of Congress are nominated and elected, with some of these changes incorporated into constitutional amendments (though with just one, the Twelfth, changing the Electoral College).

It is evident that the separation of elections and partitioning of terms sustain the separation of powers. Political parties function first and foremost to organize elections, with their committees and leaders operating interdependently throughout the federal system. Just as there is no single, determinative national election, so there is no overarching political party component. The nature of the system is such that the strength of political parties is measured by their capacity to adapt to differences among regions, state regulations, elected positions, term lengths, and the policy preferences of voters. It is a mark of the maturity of the American system that the same two major parties have existed for more than 150 years.

Presidents enter the White House under dramatically different political conditions. Some serve when their party has majority status in Congress; many others face opposition party congresses. Slightly more win in close elections, several have won by a plurality of the popular vote, and a few have lost the popular vote. The way we elect the national government permits both parties to win, thus forcing presidents to work across the aisle in support of their programs.

Presidential performance is rated more and more frequently by more and more polling organizations. As a consequence, campaigning has become a permanent feature of life in the White House. At one time, the quadrennial election was the principal occasion for a public judgment of how a president was doing his job. Now ratings are rendered many times each month. Presidents respond by taking their messages directly to the people.

One-fourth of the twentieth-century presidents first entered without being elected as such. Vice presidents taking over face the special challenge initially of governing within a presidency created to serve someone else. Given that elections are by the calendar, not by the emergence of issues, a replacement president seeking electoral legitimacy must wait for the next election year—in the cases of Theodore Roosevelt and Harry Truman, nearly four years. This arrangement is yet another variation to account for in analyzing the American presidency and its place in government.

Chapter 4
Making and remaking a presidency

Presidents enter a government already hard at work. A separated powers system is bound to feature differing tenures and work habits among its institutional components. Elected officials come and go, typically in different time frames. Bureaucrats keep on administering, judges keep on judging, and lobbyists and journalists are forever, living and working alongside the rest.

A change at the top is unquestionably important, but programs and people already in place explain most of what happens in Washington. And the workload grows, as measured by programs administered and dollars spent. It was not until 1962 that national government outlays reached $100 billion. Twenty years later, outlays exceeded $700 billion; in another twenty years, in 2002, they eclipsed the $2 trillion mark, and in just a decade more, in 2012, $3.5 trillion. Ten presidents served in these fifty years, each inheriting responsibility for the growth experienced by their predecessors.

A huge bureaucracy is required to administer programs costing billions and trillions of dollars. Much of the work is done in the cabinet departments within the executive branch, each of which reports directly to the president. There were ten of these at the end of World War II in 1945, two of which (War and Navy) were soon folded into a Department of Defense. Five were added over the

- next sixty years, each one representing new or substantially enhanced federal agendas (for example, health, education, energy, and domestic security). Outlays for the Department of Health and Human Services (HHS) during the George W. Bush presidency exceeded those for the whole federal government during the Carter presidency. Passage of the Affordable Care Act in the Obama presidency resulted in substantial further expansion in HHS.

Incoming presidents are expected to take charge of this leviathan. They will be held accountable for what takes place in an ever-changing labyrinth of federal units, programs, rules, standards, and procedures, and ties to other domestic and foreign governments. As newly elected presidents ponder the tasks of settling in, they observe others moving out—those with experience in assuming responsibility for the permanent, stay-in-Washington, government employees. Since new presidents and their aides are mostly of a different party from those leaving, little is said in passing. The new team has to learn on the job. And their job is to make a presidency effective enough to accept responsibility for what happens in government. The following is some of what must be done.

Removing the caps

Picture several triangles bounded within one large triangle. Now imagine the caps are removed from the triangles, thus forming trapezoids. Those geometric images convey what happens with a change at the top. The White House empties out, as do the offices of departmental and agency leaders. The president has a constitutional responsibility to fill many of these positions "by and with the Advice and Consent of the Senate" (Art. II, Sec. 2). During much of the nineteenth century, patronage, the appointment of partisans, extended well down into the departments and agencies. A professional civil service was created with the passage of the Pendleton Act (1883), thereafter limiting appointments to the top leadership positions.

The president makes several bundles of appointments. Among the most important are the White House staff, cabinet and subcabinet positions, agency heads and other top-level positions, regulatory commissioners, board memberships, and ambassadors and consuls. Federal judicial appointments are also vested in the president but await vacancies as these judges have life terms. There is no wholesale exit of federal judges with the election of a new president. Presidents also "have the Power to fill up all Vacancies that may happen during the Recess of the Senate" (Art. II, Sec. 2), a provision permitting the president temporarily to appoint officials whose nominations are being delayed in the Senate.

Patronage was widespread during the nation's first one hundred years, and it is still dominant in major policy positions as well as with a president's personal staff. Thus it is expected that presidents will appoint those who have demonstrated support for the party and its leader. In recent decades, however, there have been calls for presidents to appoint at least one member of the other party to the cabinet. Most post–World War II presidents have done so. Thus, for example, Senator William Cohen (R-Maine) served as secretary of defense in the administration of Democrat Bill Clinton; former Representative Norman Mineta (D-California) was appointed secretary of transportation by Republican President George W. Bush (Mineta was secretary of commerce for President Clinton); and Bush's secretary of defense, Robert Gates, was nominated by Democrat President Obama to stay in that position in his presidency.

Gender, racial, and ethnic diversity have only recently been standards for evaluating a cabinet. From 1945 to 1977 (Truman through Nixon-Ford), 97 percent of the cabinet secretaries were Caucasian men. Eisenhower appointed one woman, Johnson selected an African American man, and Ford chose a woman and an African American man. Each of these appointments was a midterm replacement or the leader of a newly created department.

The original cabinets of all four presidents in this period were exclusively white and male.

Cabinets from 1977 to 1989 had somewhat more diversity. Carter appointed three women, including one African American. Two of the three were in the original cabinet. Reagan appointed two women, one African American male, and one Hispanic American male. The African American was in the original cabinet.

Since 1989, diversity in cabinet appointments is a standard by which presidential appointments have been evaluated. Seventy-six percent of diversity appointments from 1945 to 2005 were made in this third period: George H. W. Bush made six such appointments, Clinton sixteen, and George W. Bush thirteen. Caucasian males dominated the first and second periods (97 and 87 percent, respectively) but made up just 57 percent of the third, a dramatic shift.

The number of diversity appointments to the original cabinet also increased substantially: The first Bush appointed three, Clinton eight, and the second Bush seven. In Clinton's case, white males were in the minority. They represented half of the second Bush cabinet. There was no reason to expect a reversal of this trend and, indeed, in 2009 President Obama made eight such appointments, often also making diverse appointments as replacements through his terms.

In another important development, diversity appointments began to be made for top-tier cabinet posts in the Clinton, second Bush, and Obama presidencies. Clinton appointed the first women as attorney general (Janet Reno) and secretary of state (Madeleine Albright). The second Bush appointed the first African American male and female as successive secretaries of state (Colin Powell followed by Condoleezza Rice) and the first Hispanic American as attorney general (Alberto Gonzalez). Obama appointed the first African American male and female as attorneys general (Eric Holder followed by Loretta Lynch).

5. President Reagan meeting with his cabinet in the Cabinet Room of the White House.

From campaigning to governing

Campaigning differs from governing. One presidential aide explained campaigning as a "one-ring circus," focused as it is on the candidate and a fixed day when a winner is declared. Government, by contrast, is a "thousand-ring circus."

Because the two activities are different does not mean they are unrelated. A presidential campaign determines which team will govern and influences how it will do so. Campaigns typically offer competing policy priorities or policy proposals where candidates agree on priorities. Candidates and their staffs create and manage a national organization and often intersect congressional and gubernatorial campaigns. Thus, candidates have an opportunity to learn about policy themes, preferences of others, capabilities of staff, and organizational effectiveness. It is in these respects that campaigning has the potential of preparing the winner to govern.

It is also the case that governing influences the campaign. Candidates conduct issue searches in the course of their travels.

Most issues emerge from what government is currently doing. For example, the 2004 presidential reelection campaign focused on the war on terrorism and in Iraq, home security, energy resources, Social Security, deficits, and taxes, all issues treated during George W. Bush's first term. The president interpreted his narrow win as an endorsement for his record in governing, thus promising more of the same during his second term.

By contrast, the 2008 campaign was an open election, with no incumbent seeking reelection. It occurred in the midst of a dramatic financial and economic crisis, referred to as the "great recession." The calamity displaced many of the issues forming the campaign agendas of the two candidates and was an unwelcome priority for governing by President-elect Obama, who had to reorder his intended agenda to first address the crisis.

Meanwhile, members of Congress conduct mostly separate campaigns, with issues customized to their state and local constituencies. The effect of presidents and congresses applying the lessons of campaigns to governing sets new agendas for the next election. These two functions—governing and campaigning—are truly and continually interrelated, just as one might expect in a representative democracy.

At one time presidents were reluctant to travel extensively to build support for their programs. A notable exception was the national tour of Woodrow Wilson in favor of the League of Nations in 1919. More common were fundraising trips and radio or television addresses. President Johnson observed, "Sometimes...the only way to reach the papers and the people was to pick a fight with the Congress, to say mean words and show my temper." Mostly he believed he should "work from within" because going outside might alienate members of Congress.

But in 1965 Johnson had the advantages of vast experience on Capitol Hill, a landslide win in 1964, and huge Democratic majorities in Congress. No subsequent president has had such a favorable political position. As a result, and with developments in communication, presidents have increasingly reached out to the public in building support. To aid in this task, presidents bring campaign consultants into office with them. These campaign-oriented aides are the subject of criticism. Why? They represent a fusion of campaigning and governing that many analysts believe should be separate.

Getting started: the transition

Presidents-elect have approximately ten weeks to form and prepare their presidencies. In that time they set policy priorities; make critical appointments; establish connections with Congress, the bureaucracy, the press, and other governments; and prepare to move into empty offices in the White House and other government buildings assigned to the executive branch. It is an enormously complex undertaking, one commonly involving a switch of parties when a new president is elected (eight party switches of nine transitions in the post–World War II period). Setting priorities normally follows from what was proposed during the campaign. After all, campaigns are about agendas. They form the basis of the overall debate.

It is true, however, that elections by the calendar rather than issue emergence can result in substantial variation in the sequence of priorities. No one doubted that ending the war in Vietnam was a priority for Nixon in 1968, or that energy and government ethics took precedence for Carter in 1976. The economy was paramount for Reagan in 1980 and again for Clinton in 1992 ("The economy, stupid" was a campaign theme). Much less clear were the priorities for George H. W. Bush in 1988 when the campaign was criticized for lacking issues or for George W. Bush in 2000 when several issues were debated but no one issue stood out with the public as a priority. The second Bush himself designated tax cuts as paramount.

Having a clear theme is typically a distinct advantage in transitioning into the government because it sets the purpose and direction of a presidency. An exception is when an event like the 2008 financial disaster struck during the general election campaign. The effect was to deprioritize many of the agenda items on Obama's campaign platform in favor of immediate action to stimulate the economy. George W. Bush remained as the incumbent president during the critical ten weeks of the transition as Obama formed his government and proposed a package to deal with the emergency, and a Democratic Congress acted in advance of the inauguration.

Media attention during the transition understandably focuses on critical appointments. There is strong interest in filling in the boxes, those key cabinet posts and the principal staff aides to the president. The transition is an anxious time for many campaign aides who anticipate appointments. And interest runs high among groups that do business with the government, as well as congressional committees and their staffs who will be working with the White House and cabinet departments.

Certain practices and sequences have developed for making appointments, most of which are effectively implemented if there has been transition planning prior to the election itself. Among these customs are the following: select an appointments chief with federal government experience, act fast, appoint White House staff and major cabinet posts (State, Treasury, Defense, Justice) as early as feasible, quickly settle the futures of close advisers, let appointments speak for policy, and separate the functions of dismantling the campaign from those of managing appointments.

Taken together these practices amount to clear-headed and logical planning for a change in administrations in which program and personnel are sufficiently coordinated as to convey a well-defined sense of mission. Measured by these standards, the Kennedy (1960), Reagan (1980), and George W. Bush (2000) transitions received high marks by analysts; the Carter (1976),

Table 4.1 Cabinet Departments

Department	Date created
State	1789
Treasury	1789
Defense	1789 as War; 1798 as Navy; 1947 as Defense
Justice	1792 as Attorney General; 1870 as Justice
Interior	1849
Agriculture	1889 as cabinet level
Labor	1913 (originally Commerce and Labor, 1903)
Commerce	1913 (originally Commerce and Labor, 1903)
Health and Human Services	1953 as Health, Education, and Welfare; 1979 as Health and Human Services
Housing and Urban Development	1965
Transportation	1966
Energy	1977
Education	1979
Veterans Affairs	1988
Homeland Security	2002

Source: Compiled from information in *The United States Government Manual, 2005–2006* (Washington, DC: Government Printing Office, 2005).

George H. W. Bush (1988), and especially Clinton (1992) transitions had low marks. A smooth transition does not guarantee an effective presidency, but it does make it more likely to get off to a good start.

6. Transition from one generation to the next—Eisenhower to Kennedy.

"Innocent until nominated" is how C. Boyden Gray, counsel to the first President Bush, described the appointment process. Scholars argue that its complexity and invasiveness deter high-quality candidates from entering government. Nominees are subject to background checks by the Federal Bureau of Investigation, elaborate financial disclosure forms, reviews by Senate committee staffs, questioning in confirmation hearings, and scrutiny by the media and interest groups. All of this examination takes time. Delay in filling critical posts, especially at the subcabinet level, complicates an already challenging task for a new president in assuming responsibility for governing.

Partisanship too can add to the trials of a new administration. It is generally conceded that presidents should be able to appoint the people they want. Therefore, the Senate consents to most appointments. More often than not in recent decades, however, the president has had to get consent from a Senate controlled by the other party (the case at different times for Nixon, Ford, Reagan, George H. W. Bush, Clinton, George W. Bush, and Obama). Accordingly, presidents have had to consider the possibility that a nominee will be rejected, as, for example, was the high-profile nomination of former Senator John Tower (R-Texas) to be secretary of defense in the first Bush cabinet. Remarkably, many of his former colleagues in the Senate voted against Tower. An interesting note is that next in line for George H. W. Bush was Richard Cheney, who later served with Bush's son as vice president.

Although of a different order, judicial appointments, too, have come to be very contentious. These appointments are not a part of building a presidency. Rather, they represent an exercise of the president's constitutional authority in the case of "Judges of the supreme Court" (Art. II, Sec. 1) and as designated by law in the cases of judges for "inferior Courts" (Art. III, Sec. 1). These appointments are to fill vacancies in the third branch and are essentially life terms, not coincident with a president's time in office.

As with executive appointments, most of the president's judicial choices are approved. But split-party control between the president and the Senate has made the process of "advice and consent" increasingly stressful, particularly for the courts of appeals and the Supreme Court. Appointments may be held up in the Senate Committee on the Judiciary or, rarely, defeated on the Senate floor. In the 108th Congress (2003–05), the minority-party Democrats employed the filibuster to thwart several of George W. Bush's appointments to the courts of appeals, a practice halted at least temporarily by a bipartisan agreement in the 109th Congress (2005–07).

Turnover: remaking a presidency

Having formed a presidency, achieved the consent of the Senate for the cabinet, and fitted the new team into the permanent government of long-serving bureaucrats, a high incumbent-return Congress, and life-term judges, presidents can only hope their appointees will cohere and serve out a full term. But there are no guarantees. Those appointed typically come from very different backgrounds. In parliamentary systems the cabinet is typically made up of ministers with similar political experiences—mostly as members of parliament. Not so in the separated system of the United States. Cabinet secretaries have varied backgrounds in the public and private spheres. For example, the first cabinets of Clinton, George W. Bush, and Obama were drawn from business and banking, law, Congress, education, state and local governments, and the military. Most will not have worked together in the past; a few may not even be well acquainted with the president. The challenge is to ensure that a disparate set of department heads supports the president's programs and knows how to put them in place.

The White House staff typically does have a common political experience, as most will have been active in the campaign just ended. But it is rare for these campaign aides to be appointed to the first cabinet. They are, however, intimately familiar with the president's programs and how they were conceived and formed during the campaign. They are, therefore, well qualified to monitor how and whether proposals are being processed and promoted within the departments and agencies; this is certainly true for those with experience enough to know their way around Washington.

It is not uncommon for conflicts to develop between these staff members and department and agency heads, or for both groups to be at odds with senior career bureaucrats. A president's loyalists sometimes refer to presidential appointees "going native" as they settle into their positions. The concern is they will express more allegiance to existing programs than to the president's agenda for change.

Serving a president is a temporary job. After all, the Twenty-second Amendment sets a two-term limitation on presidential service.

Few cabinet secretaries serve two full terms, and just ten have done so since the ratification of the term-limitation amendment in 1951: Eisenhower, two; Kennedy-Johnson, three; Reagan, one; and Clinton, four. Turnover is high, though variable. The median number of months served by cabinet secretaries for two-term administrations (including those when a vice president took over, such as Kennedy-Johnson and Nixon-Ford) varies from forty-eight months for Clinton's eight years to twenty-four months for the eight years of Nixon-Ford. The Nixon and Ford presidencies had a total of forty-three cabinet secretarial appointments; Eisenhower had just twenty. Remarkably, there were five attorneys general and five secretaries of labor serving Nixon and Ford, an average of just over nineteen months for each appointee in these two sets.

What explains these significant differences in turnover? Certainly a shift in presidents (as with Kennedy's death and Nixon's resignation) can be expected to produce turnover as the takeover presidents eventually bring in their own teams. In Nixon's case, however, there was a pattern of high turnover even before he resigned. Appointing people to the right job at the start appears to be important in their retention. A good working relationship with the president and the White House staff is also essential. Even when these conditions are met, however, turnover is relatively high. The jobs are demanding, testimony on Capitol Hill is frequent, criticism is inevitable, and the pay is relatively low. Thus, high-profile people often prefer to return to more rewarding positions in the private sphere.

The Clinton and second Bush presidencies suggest that change may be under way. The Clinton cabinet had one of the lowest turnover rates of any eight-year presidency in the twentieth century and the highest number of secretaries serving the full eight years. The George W. Bush cabinet set a modern record for the fewest resignations in a first term, a turnover of just two cabinet secretaries—one voluntarily, one involuntarily. That

record was then followed by another—the highest number of
changes in the cabinet between the first and second terms.
Perhaps turnover in the future will be lessened, with greater
stability a result. That outcome is surely to be welcomed because
frequent changes at the top result in having to reestablish
connections between the bureaucracy and the White House,
Congress, the states, and other governments.

First and second terms

First and second terms are very different. The pressures are
intense in the first term to make appointments that will meet the
expectations of campaign workers and contributors, members of
Congress, interest groups, party organizations, and the media.
Each appointment is evaluated for what it reveals about the new
presidency in policy and political terms.

Second-term appointments also receive attention, but the
situation is markedly different. Certain key personnel may decide
to continue, the president has somewhat greater flexibility in
filling vacancies, and the pool of potential nominees will include
people who either have experience in the department or agency
or have earned the president's confidence in performing other
related jobs.

Nine presidents were reelected (1896–2012): McKinley, Wilson,
Franklin Roosevelt (three times), Eisenhower, Nixon, Reagan,
Clinton, George W. Bush, and Obama. Their records show that
renewal of the cabinet at the point of reelection is a modern
phenomenon. The first set of four—McKinley, Wilson, FDR in his
second term, and Eisenhower—made no changes in their cabinets
at the point of their reelections. FDR did have a single change in
each of his second and third reelections (1940 and 1944).

The second set—Nixon, Reagan, Clinton, George W. Bush, and
Obama—made major changes at the point of reelection. In 1972,

Nixon asked for the resignations of the entire White House staff and the cabinet. "There are no sacred cows....We will tear up the pea patch," Nixon reportedly said to his staff. Six changes were made in the cabinet (50 percent turnover), and the staff was reorganized. Reagan matched Nixon in making six changes; Clinton appointed five new cabinet secretaries, and George W. Bush set an all-time record with eight changes, subsequently matched by Obama. In the latter four instances, the shifts were explained more by preferences of the cabinet secretaries than by a Nixon-style house cleaning. Still the effect was a renewal of each of the four presidencies, with an average turnover of nearly half following reelections.

It is frequently stated that there is a second-term curse, suggesting that reelected presidents are bound to fail. The contention is that much of a president's program is enacted in the first term, Washington insiders consider a second-term president a "lame duck," and a laxness develops that encourages scandal. A brief review of the historical record suggests that what happens in the second term is more circumstantially than historically determined. The number of reelected presidents in the modern era is small. It becomes smaller as one reviews each case.

McKinley was assassinated, and Wilson had a severe stroke, both events occurring within a year of their reelections. FDR was reelected three times, thus making it difficult to argue that he was cursed. Nixon resigned in the second year of his second term as a consequence of the Watergate investigation. What of the others?

Eisenhower, Reagan, and Clinton suffered from scandals of very different sorts. For Eisenhower, his chief of staff, Sherman Adams, accepted gifts from a businessman, Bernard Goldfine, who was being investigated for violations of Federal Trade Commission regulations. Adams was accused of aiding Goldfine. Reagan's White House used profits from covert sales of arms to Iran to support the "contras" seeking to overthrow the Nicaraguan government. Clinton's personal behavior with a White House intern, Monica Lewinsky, was the basis of scandal during his second term. An ongoing investigation directed by special counsel Kenneth Starr incorporated the Lewinsky matter. The president was impeached in the House of Representatives but his trial in the Senate did not result in his removal.

Did these second-term scandals wreck the presidencies in each case? The evidence is not conclusive enough to generalize about a "curse." Several factors are relevant: public job approval ratings of the president by expert analysts, midterm election results, and production of major legislation. Here are the facts: Job approval ratings for Eisenhower and Reagan were declining prior to each scandal, then increased to the end of their terms. Midterm losses were substantial for Republicans in 1958, primarily due to an economic recession; Republican losses were slight in 1986 but, in any event, the election occurred before the Iran-contra revelations and scandal. And passage of major legislation was greater in the second than the first term for both Eisenhower and Reagan.

Clinton's scandal is much more personal and possibly had more effect. Yet his approval ratings dipped only moderately, then rebounded. Democrats actually gained House seats in 1998, with no net loss in the Senate. There was, however, substantially less major legislation in the second term over the first. And the president was the second in history to be impeached.

That leaves George W. Bush and Obama among post–World War II reelected presidents. Bush started his second term rather audaciously in spite of his narrow victory—the smallest reelection margin since Woodrow Wilson's in 1916. Social Security reform led an ambitious agenda, but it did not make it to the floor in either the Republican House or Senate. Meanwhile, the president authorized a "surge" in the unpopular war in Iraq, with modest positive effects for his status. However, poor management and wretched images of the devastating effects of hurricane Katrina were highly negative for the president. The calamity of the "great recession" in the fall of 2008 left the Bush presidency mostly counting the days until it ended. The president's job approval ratings had plummeted from the highest ever recorded during his leadership in responding to the 9/11 disaster to among the lowest recorded for any president. Bush may well have concluded that he was cursed.

Obama was reelected in 2012 substantially more comfortably than Bush, though with a smaller popular vote than he received in 2008 and failing to be accompanied by Democrats winning back a majority in the House of Representatives. Like Bush, he announced a bold agenda, essentially ignoring the return of a Republican majority in the House. Little of what he wanted was enacted as partisanship dominated congressional action. Furthermore, the launching of the Affordable Care Act was notably subpar in execution. In the 2014 midterm election Republicans won a majority in the Senate, increased their numbers in the House, and won more state houses. It was among the most successful opposition party victories ever in a second midterm election, further limiting President Obama's political capital in Congress.

These mixed results make it difficult to take a broad view of second terms. Scandals are not that closely associated with either job-approval ratings or election outcomes. Major legislation can be and is enacted during second terms, sometimes in greater amounts than in first terms. A more supportable conclusion than that implied by a second-term curse is that a host of variables combine to influence the workings and production of a separated powers system, much as one would expect from the way the Founders designed the government. It is useful to be reminded that the original design had no term limit and therefore no structural basis for a "lame-duck" president. However, the experiences of the recent line of three reelected presidents— Clinton, George W. Bush, and Obama—since Jefferson, Madison, and Monroe invites caution in designing a second term.

Institutional dynamism

The presidency is a dynamic institution, one constantly being shaped and reshaped. Two major factors explain this vitality, both associated with its democratic base. First, presidents enter and leave, actually rather frequently as it happens. They are given latitude in forming their presidencies within certain bounds. If reelected they have the option of reshaping, perhaps revitalizing, their organization and agenda. Second, the presidency is purposely and historically representative. Accordingly, one may expect responsiveness to events in the form of organizational and programmatic adjustments. Other elections, notably those for Congress, are sensitive as representative bodies, to these same events—a reality influencing presidential decisions.

Institutional dynamism does not imply instability or radical change. Indeed, the separation of powers is designed to thwart dramatic reshaping of the structure and organization of the executive branch. Presidents do make adjustments that may then be incorporated into future White House operations. The presidency has undergone evolutionary change since the end of World War II. Typically, however, the shifts reflect social, economic, and technological changes in the nation, much as one would expect in a representative democracy.

Chapter 5
Connecting to and leading the government

The opening sentence of Article II, "The executive Power shall be vested in a President of the United States of America," might well have included the following phrase: "who will be responsible for connecting to the rest of the government." The Founders created a government of parts. As the only nationally elected leader and chief of the bureaucratic branch, it was inevitable that the president would be held accountable for all parts. That fact alone is a stimulus for presidential attentiveness to what happens throughout government.

And what a government it has become. *The United States Government Manual* lists the following units for the executive branch (apart from the Executive Office of the President [EOP]): fifteen cabinet departments; fifty-nine independent establishments and government corporations; fifty-one boards, commissions, and committees; four quasi-official agencies; and numerous international, regional, and financial multi- and bilateral organizations. And these agencies are but the tips of many icebergs. For example, the Department of Defense has three departments, one for each of the services, sixteen agencies, and numerous commands and field activities. The recently created Department of Homeland Security has two assistant secretaries, seven directors, one deputy secretary, five undersecretaries, and a commandant of the Coast Guard. There are independent organizational units in the executive branch on futures trading, product safety, arts and humanities, postal rates, and transportation safety, to name but a few.

Organizations manage people, millions of people in the case of the national government. Total federal employment, civilian and military, approaches 4 million—approximately the size of the city of Los Angeles. The number of elected officials in Washington, by contrast, is very small. The number of legislators increased with the addition of states for the Senate and the increase in population for the House of Representatives until the latter was capped at 435 in 1911. The number on the executive side stayed at one president and one vice president. Now look at the number of employees: millions to be managed by the two elected executives; more than 30,000 for 535 members of Congress.

Table 5.1 Federal Employment, 2014

Branch		Employees	
Executive: Civilian		2,663,000	
Executive: Military		1,459,000	
Legislative		31,300	
Judicial		34,500	
Total		4,187,800	
Elected Officials	1789		2014
Executive	2		2
Legislative: House	65 (13 states)		435 (50 states)
Legislative: Senate	26 (13 states)		100 (50 states)
Judicial	0		0

Sources: *Statistical Abstract of the United States* (Washington, DC: Government Printing Office) and Office of Personnel Management sources.

But the number of federal employees has actually decreased in recent years—for several reasons. More of the work of the federal government is now done at the state and local levels, where the number of employees has increased by 40 percent since 1995 (now approaching 20 million). Also, work formerly done by government employees is now often contracted out to private firms. And military service is now voluntary (not conscripted) and high tech. These developments reduce the number of employees but increase management and accountability issues. Federal programs such as Medicaid or crime control may be directed at lower levels of government, but the president will still be held responsible for results.

Increasing costs and mounting deficits likewise justify White House awareness of the governing apparatus and being knowledgeable of how and where money is spent. The numbers are staggering and appear to escalate in spite of efforts to control expenditures. Previously unimagined deficits have contributed to an overall public debt of epic proportions. Government expenditures are in the billions and trillions of dollars. Money coming in actually exceeded outlays in 2000, a remarkable achievement representing an economic boom at the end of the century. Even so, the gross federal debt continued to rise as deficits in other years soared. Tax receipts grew sixfold between 1980 and 2014, but outlays grew eightfold. Yet outlays as a percentage of Gross Domestic Product (GDP), a standard measure of the economy, have remained near 20 percent. More troubling is the mounting total debt, as it continues to climb into the trillions and has grown from one-third of GDP to a phenomenal 18 trillion, exceeding the GDP.

How much is a trillion? It is very hard to illustrate in human terms, but someone once calculated the weight in dollar bills of the debt when it first passed $1.5 trillion as equivalent to fifteen aircraft carriers, twelve destroyers, two battleships, two cruisers, and seventeen smaller ships combined. At this writing, the gross

Table 5.2 Receipts, Outlays, Deficits, and Debt (in billions of dollars)

Budget	Year			
Features	1980	1990	2000	2014
Receipts	517.1	1,032.0	2,025.2	3,002.4
Outlays	590.9	1,253.2	1,788.8	3,777.8
Surplus or deficit	−73.8	−221.2	+236.4	−484,6
Outlays as % of GDP*	21.7	21.8	18.4	20.1
Gross federal debt	909.0	3,206.3	5,628.7	17,794.4
Debt as % of GDP*	33.4	55.9	58.0	107.1

* GDP = Gross Domestic Product

Sources: *Statistical Abstract of the United States 2004–2005* (Washington, DC: Government Printing Office), and various budget documents.

debt is on its way to 20 trillion. You can do the math. Talk about the need for Weight Watchers!

For present purposes, the numbers point up the urgency for presidents to reach into the permanent government in their efforts to exercise executive power. Existing programs have the force of the organization that administers them and the clienteles they serve. A new president is already behind schedule in managing this behemoth. The outgoing president and staff formed the budget in place and prepared the next fiscal year's spending and taxing plans. Yet the effects of spending and implementing what is on the books soon will be on the new leader's "watch."

Connecting to whom?

To whom or what must presidents connect? However much they are held responsible for what happens, the fact is that presidential direction and control over different parts of the government vary substantially. For some segments presidents hire and fire, reorganize to an extent, and exercise budgetary power. Other segments have differing degrees of independence, ranging from their own sources of legitimacy to the strength of public or clientele support. The categories—from most White House control to least—are these: cabinet departments and other agencies with appointments coterminous with the president's term or at his pleasure, independent agencies with overlapping and lengthy terms, the other branches of the national government, and even the media, and other governments and international organizations.

Cabinet departments and major agencies

It is generally conceded that presidents have the right to manage the large departments and agencies. After all, presidents have the gold standard of legitimacy in a democracy—their election. Presidents appoint secretaries, administrators, and directors who are then expected to put into practice presidential policy preferences. Centralized budget control and clearance of program initiatives are levers that presidents use to enforce their decisions. Those who fail to satisfy the president can be removed. Recent examples: Secretary of Defense Les Aspin was removed by President Clinton early in his presidency, Secretary of the Treasury Paul O'Neill was fired by President George W. Bush, Secretary of Defense Chuck Hagel was eased out by President Barack Obama.

Independent commissions

Congress has established several commissions for policy areas judged to be better placed beyond partisan influences. Most deal with economic and regulatory issues: securities and exchange, banking, interest rates, trade, shipping, communications, labor relations. Each of these issues is served by an independent commission. Paramount among the groups is the Federal Reserve

System, the "Fed," for the impact of its interest rate decisions on the economy. Presidents appoint the commissioners but cannot normally remove them; their terms are staggered so as to provide continuity and usually exceed a president's single term of four years. Bipartisan representation is required on these commissions, with neither party permitted to have an advantage of more than one. Presidents can influence policy through their appointments, but often the greater threats to their independence are the consequences of their favoring the very industries they are charged to regulate.

The other branches

Life terms for federal judges are the principal basis for the independence of the judiciary, bolstered by the common belief that elected officials should not influence individual court decisions. Presidents have their chance to affect the direction of courts with their constitutional prerogative of nominating judges, as do senators during the "advice and consent" process in that chamber. Federal court appointments have become increasingly contentious in recent decades with the frequency of split-party government and narrow margins between the parties in the Senate. Furthermore, nominees for judgeships presumed to be of one philosophical persuasion have, once seated, turned out quite differently (for example, on the Supreme Court, Byron White, a Kennedy appointee, was thought to be moderate to liberal yet served as a moderate to conservative justice; John Paul Stevens, a Ford appointee, and David Souter, a George H. W. Bush appointee, proved just the opposite).

There is no expectation that presidents will cease influencing Congress. Rather, the challenge is to establish relationships with elaborate and differentiated organizations in the House and Senate. The committees and subcommittees in each chamber are an approximate replication of the programmatic structure in the executive (for example, the Department of Defense and the House and Senate Committees on Armed Services). Therefore, connections already exist between the bureaus and their counterpart committees, two of the three legs of what has been termed "cozy little triangles" (the third leg being the private and clientele interests affected by the issue at hand). Somehow presidents who want to change policies have to find the means to override these lasting associations by developing close ties of their own with lawmakers (as well as committee and subcommittee permanent staff).

Just as important is the need to fashion strong relationships with party leaders, including knowledge of what these leaders need by way of White House support to build majorities for or against legislation. In some instances, the president's party in Congress will have just experienced years of policy strife with an opposition party president. For example, when Kennedy and Clinton were inaugurated, Democrats had been in the majority in the House and Senate for six years during the Eisenhower and Reagan-Bush presidencies respectively; as Obama was sworn in, Democrats had led both chambers for the last two years of the George W. Bush presidency. Likewise, Republicans had had House and Senate majorities for six years during the Clinton presidency when Bush entered office. Having honed their skills at opposing the White House, the president's party on Capitol Hill had to become cheerleaders—not always an easy transformation, yet one that may be eased by an adroit presidential staff.

Media

There is a perpetual tension between two vital institutions: the presidency and the press. As Gary Wills has noted, "Sooner or later, all presidents blame the problems on the media, and they are right. The press and the president are linked in a natural enmity. They need each other and they resent that." The two institutions are naturally competitive, even combative. Presidents are representatives of the people by virtue of having been elected.

Reporters believe it is their professional, even constitutional, First Amendment obligation to inform the people of presidential doings. There are few more sensitive relationships in national politics. The White House press corps is a group of reporters from the print and electronic media who work in the president's house and follow the president's travel schedule. The White House communications operations provide daily briefings and manage alternative outlets for informing the public of national policy decisions. The press secretary becomes a familiar spokesperson for presidential policy decisions.

Other governments

The federal government is intricately connected to governance in the fifty states and thousands of localities. According to the Bureau of the Census count, there are more than 87,500 local governmental units (counties, municipalities, townships, and special districts), the overwhelming number receiving and spending federal funds.

Federal grants-in-aid to state and local governments total hundreds of billions of dollars, constituting approximately one-third of all expenditures by those governments. A huge proportion of this money is for Medicaid, income security, transportation, and education—programs at the core of state and local governance. Spending for some programs is growing at alarming rates, most notably for Medicaid with the passage of "Obamacare" and income security.

Presidents wishing to reduce or reform these programs have to plan carefully given the investment of the federal government in the social and economic life of states and localities. They need to take advantage of the connections between federal departments and the governments actually administering the programs in preparing proposals for change. They can be guaranteed that members of Congress, all elected from states and congressional districts, will be attentive to the effects of reforms in their districts. In fact, it is at this level that government can become very personal for individuals and families, with their responses to changes a predictable result, often as resistance. It is relevant in this regard that presidents who have served as governors (four of the six between 1976 and 2016) are more likely to be sensitive to these needs.

Connecting with foreign governments and international organizations is of a different order. Several cabinet departments (notably Commerce, Defense, Labor, and Treasury) have regular contact with counterparts in other countries, but the Department of State is the primary agency for maintaining relations outside the United States. Presidents appoint ambassadors, who become their personal representatives, but most of those staffing the embassies and other diplomatic missions around the world are career Foreign Service personnel, with one at each location designated as Chief of Mission. Likewise, other countries maintain embassies in Washington, DC, essentially their place of contact in the United States.

As is evident, the president's reach into these organizations, branches, and governments is achieved through appointments and feedback. However, tension between appointees from the outside and long-serving bureaucrats on the inside is common and understandable. Often the friction is between long-serving experts and limited-term politicians. The challenge for presidents is to take advantage of bureaucratic experience in formulating and promoting their programs.

Accomplishing this goal can be especially difficult in foreign and national security policies. Domestic bureaucracies are located mostly in the United States; foreign and national security policy bureaucracies are located in the United States and throughout the world. Further, differences in attitude and style typically arise between diplomats and the military, thus creating an added form of tension to be managed by presidents.

Can it be done?

Public administration scholars question the extent to which presidents are prepared to manage the executive branch. They typically lack skills, interest, or both. To serve actively as "chief" executive, presidents must rely on others. For decades they lacked sufficient assistance in this regard.

The problem of getting more help for the president was officially recognized in 1937 with a report from a President's Committee on Administrative Management. Its conclusion: "The President needs help." Two years later the Executive Office of the President (EOP) was created. In essence, this action produced an institutional home for units to facilitate information gathering and policy control. Over time the EOP was bound to enlarge its functions and staff, not unlike the bureaucracy it was created to manage. What began as a few advisers has grown into many hundreds of staff organized into the major policy areas represented by federal government programs. The present-day EOP organizationally is a microcosm of the permanent executive branch.

Just two of the EOP's organizational units were a part of the office in 1939—the White House Office (WHO) and the Office of Management and Budget (OMB, originally called the Bureau of the Budget). Two exceedingly important councils were created in the immediate post–World War II period: the Council of Economic Advisers (CEA) and the National Security Council (NSC). The remaining six were established from 1963 forward.

All the major policy areas—the economy, national security and foreign policy, trade, environmental issues, science and technology, the domestic agenda, and the budget—are covered by these EOP units. They serve several purposes. Some are advisory only (CEA, Council on Environmental Quality, and Office of

Table 5.3 Executive Office of the President (EOP)

Unit	Created By	Year
White House Office	Executive Order	1939
Office of the Vice President	Constitutional Official	1960s–1970s staff growth
Council of Economic Advisers	Employment Act	1946
Council on Environmental Quality	National Environmental Protection Act	1969
National Security Council	National Security Act	1947
Office of Administration	Executive Order	1977
Office of Management and Budget	Reorganization Plan No. 1 (as the Bureau of the Budget)	1939
Office of National Drug Control Policy	National Narcotics Leadership Act	1988
Office of Policy Development		
—Domestic Policy Council	Executive Order	1993
—National Economic Council	Executive Order	1993
Office of Science and Technology Policy	National Science and Technology Policy Organization and Priorities Act	1971
Office of the US Trade Representative	Executive Order	1963
Council on Women and Girls	Executive Order	2009

Science and Technology Policy). Others have responsibilities for coordinating major policy decisions (NSC, the Domestic Policy and National Economic Councils). Two of the units have policymaking functions: the Offices of National Drug Control

Policy and the US Trade Representative. The Office of Administration performs primarily housekeeping functions.

That leaves OMB and the WHO, the most important units of all. OMB is a high-level coordinating agency. Its list of functions is awesome: prepare and administer the budget, review government effectiveness, recommend organizational changes, clear legislative proposals from departments and agencies, evaluate government performance, and develop regulatory reform proposals.

Presidents vary in the extent to which they rely on OMB, but none believes a presidency can work effectively without its experience and expertise. Since 1974, Congress has had a counterpart agency, the Congressional Budget Office, and House and Senate Committees on the Budget. These creations have facilitated interactions between the branches on this vital function.

The inner circle

The WHO is the inner circle of White House aides, those on whom the president relies for in-house advice and counsel. These people constitute the "team," those whom the president trusts, often because they have fought the election wars and/or served with the president in his prior positions. Many of them will have come to Washington with the president, for example, Georgians who served with Carter, Californians with Reagan, Arkansans with Clinton, Texans with George W. Bush, all former governors, and Chicagoans with former Illinois US Senator Obama. At best, these aides come to think like the presidents they serve and to understand what is in their president's best interests. At worst, they become arrogant "know-it-alls," serving the president and the country poorly. Bradley H. Patterson, with fourteen years of service for three presidents, refers to the WHO as "the ring of power."

Close identity with the president can protect, even enhance, presidential power by enabling the staff to be sensitive to the future effects of current decisions. Most effective are those aides who warn as well as inform. Position, the status of being president, does not make the holder supreme. Therefore, staff can be enormously helpful by being critical as well as analytical. Least helpful is for staff persons to serve their own egos, anxious to strengthen their personal careers.

Presidential appointments to the WHO are not subject to Senate confirmation given the personal nature of staff functions and structure. Presidents have wide discretion in judging how to organize White House operations. Some, such as Kennedy and Carter, preferred open access to the Oval Office, not wishing to have a chief of staff. Others, such as Eisenhower and Nixon preferred more control through a chief of staff. Reagan worked initially with a "troika," although one of the three, James Baker, was the chief of staff. Clinton, both Bushes, and Obama wanted both: a chief of staff and substantial access for other aides. Not surprisingly given the demands of the job, turnover has become rather high for White House chiefs of staff

The policy issues brought into the White House Office will also vary, depending on the national agenda and the preferences of the president. George W. Bush wanted homeland security and faith-based and community initiatives managed in the WHO. For Clinton, "reinventing government" was a priority. Lyndon Johnson wanted the poverty program to be located in the White House for the express purpose of stressing the importance of the new program. Health care, climate change, and, later, immigration were crucial for Obama. Of course, national security is a standard priority agenda issue for all inner circles.

The management functions are more settled though they continue to expand. It is the responsibility of many of these aides to establish and maintain the connections with the president. Apart from the internal management functions (for example, chief of staff, staff secretary, personnel), most activities involve liaison

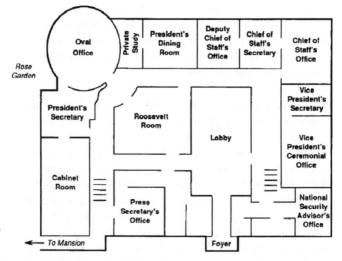

7. The West Wing of the White House, where the president and the inner circle work.

functions with Congress, media, cabinet, general public, and state and local governments. In fact, much of the work of the WHO can be labeled "communications." Presidents work at initiating and maintaining contact and conversations with governmental and public audiences, a task made more complex by dramatic changes in how information is transmitted and received. In his sixth year as president, Obama was the first to establish a Twitter account.

In 1939, President Franklin Roosevelt first appointed six staff to the newly formed WHO. Two of the six had titles. All were generalists prepared to work on whatever the president designated. The Committee on Administrative Management suggested the following qualities for these aides: "They would remain in the background, issue no orders, make no decisions, emit no public statements.... They should be possessed of high competence, great vigor, and a passion for anonymity."

It was inevitable that the staff would increase in size with the growth of government. The subtitle of Bradley Patterson's "ring of power" book is *The White House Staff and Its Expanding Role in Government*. Few would have predicted, however, by how much the staff would expand in both numbers and power. At the millennium and beyond, "titleitis" was rampant. In 2015, twenty-six staff were titled assistant to the president, fifteen deputy assistant to the president, and five special assistant to the president. Most of these aides had second titles as well—for example, chief of staff, deputy chief of staff, director, counsel, senior adviser, press secretary. "Passion for anonymity" is hardly apparent in the contemporary WHO. Furthermore, many aides become familiar public figures, often spokespersons for the administration in their area of expertise, appearing frequently on television talk shows.

Presidents often have special consultants whose formal position is unlikely to reveal the influence such persons exercise. Typically the advice of these confidants is more politically than policy oriented, but it is often difficult to separate the two. Recent advances in polling and other forms of political communication have made these positions more specialized than in the past. After Republicans captured control of Congress in 1994, President Clinton turned for help to Dick Morris, a political consultant he had worked with in the past. Morris's role at first was a secret, even to other White House staff. Later, when his role as a presidential adviser was known, Morris was a controversial figure, judged by certain White House staff to be disruptive of their work.

The position and influence of Karl Rove in the George W. Bush presidency was never covert. He was acknowledged to have been the principal political architect of Bush's campaigns for election and reelection. During the second term he was appointed deputy chief of staff in the WHO, a position with influence on policy as well as politics. Nor was the role of David Axelrod as senior adviser for politics in the Obama presidency hidden from public view. Axelrod often represented the White House in public forums, not at all remaining in the background, as recommended by the 1937–39 Committee.

The vice president

The president's first appointment in government comes before winning office, as the presidential candidate chooses a running mate who then serves as vice president. For most of history, the principal job of the vice president was to be ready to assume the presidency in case of the death, incapacity, removal, or resignation of the president. For many, the title might better have been "Vice Asterisk." Take a test: Who was FDR's first vice president? Woodrow Wilson's? More recently: Richard Nixon's first? However, nine vice presidents became presidents, and five of these subsequently ran for a full term of their own, four successfully.

Presidents do not plan to leave office involuntarily and therefore they have, in the past, typically selected running mates more to help them get elected than to help in governing later. Recent practice, however, has been to acknowledge the potential usefulness of a vice president once in office, often to strengthen a presidential weakness. For example, Carter had no Washington or congressional experience, and he chose a respected veteran—US senator, Walter Mondale, as his running mate. Lacking a background in foreign policy, Reagan chose an experienced diplomat, George H. W. Bush. Like Carter, Clinton and George W. Bush needed help on Capitol Hill and elsewhere in Washington. Clinton chose Al Gore, who had served in both the House of Representatives and the Senate. Bush selected Richard Cheney, whose service in the House of Representatives, the White House as Ford's chief of staff, and the cabinet as secretary of defense made him one of the most broadly experienced vice presidents in history. As a freshman US senator, candidate Obama

The American Presidency

turned to a senior colleague, Joseph Biden, who had served thirty-eight years in the US Senate, for help in that chamber. While in the Senate, Biden also served as chair of the Senate committees on the Judiciary and Foreign Relations.

In each of these cases, the vice president aided the president in making connections to Congress and the bureaucracy. This greater role in governance has resulted in a larger and more specialized staff for the vice president, now greater in size than those for presidents in the immediate post–World War II era. Vice President Biden's staff in 2015 included a chief of staff and two deputies, a press secretary and two deputies, a chief of staff for the "Second Lady," plus fourteen additional aides, some of whom carried the title deputy assistant to the president. Biden's predecessor, Richard Cheney, had a similar sized staff. Seldom does one expect a reduction in staff from one presidency to the next.

One consideration in promoting the active involvement of vice presidents is the extent of their own ambition to be president. It has become almost routine in the post–World War II era for vice presidents to run for the presidency. The list includes Nixon (1960 and 1968), Humphrey (1968), the first Bush (1988), and Gore (2000). Additionally, Mondale (1984) and Quayle (2000) ran after having served earlier as vice presidents. Mondale lost badly to Reagan; Quayle did not win the nomination in 2000. Of those making this effort, only George H. W. Bush won as a sitting vice president—the first to do so since Martin Van Buren in 1836. Nixon won in 1968 on his second try. Overall the record of recent vice-presidential efforts to move to the Oval Office is grim: seven tries, one win out of the box, one win on the second try.

Recognizing the unique partnership of the president and vice president, Harvard professor and foremost presidential scholar Richard E. Neustadt forwarded some "rules of thumb" to his former Harvard student, Al Gore, then running for vice president with Bill Clinton. Among the most relevant rules are these:

1. The VP reminds the P of his mortality; the P reminds the VP of his dependency.
2. The White House staff lives in the present, the VP's staff in the future.
3. The VP can't be fired, but the P can ignore, or haze him—and, if the P, then staff will too—with relative impunity.
4. The only thing more frustrating than being bypassed is to have one's advice heard, pondered, and not taken.

The working relationships between recent presidents and vice presidents have been quite strong and productive. Most vice presidents in the future may be expected to have presidential ambitions. After all, they are in a superb position to observe and to reflect on how they might have managed a decision. However, the vice president with the most responsibilities in recent decades, Richard Cheney, announced well in advance that he had no intention of running for president.

First spouses

To this point, First Spouses have been First Ladies. A common function has been that of hostess, with the fashionable Dolley Madison serving as the model. The tasks were significant but not directly related to policy or politics. As Lady Bird Johnson put it: "The First Lady is, and always has been, an unpaid public servant, elected by one person, her husband."

In contemporary times, an Office of the First Lady provides staff to assist with scheduling, travel, planning social and ceremonial events, decoration of the White House, and food service. Included among staff appointments are a chief of staff, press secretary, social secretary, and floral designer. Recently, First Ladies have also been active in designated, mostly nonpartisan, policy areas. For example: Lady Bird Johnson, beautification of public facilities; Pat Nixon, volunteerism; Rosalynn Carter, mental disabilities; Nancy Reagan, "Just Say No" to drugs; Barbara Bush, literacy; Hillary Clinton, health care; Laura Bush, childhood literacy; and Michelle Obama, childhood obesity. Again, staff has been provided for such efforts.

Eleanor Roosevelt was extraordinary in displaying independence, essentially defining herself by her spirited activities. The National First Ladies Library (NFLL) quotes her as stating: "There isn't going to be any First Lady. There is just to be plain, ordinary Mrs. Roosevelt. I never wanted to be the President's wife. And don't want it now." Because of the crippling effects of poliomyelitis on her husband, she often traveled for him, but she also emerged as a separate, highly respected public person on national and international issues; she gave speeches on social issues, wrote a weekly newspaper column, hosted a radio show, and met with troops during World War II.

In striking contrast to this model, Nancy Reagan is quoted by the NFLL on her concept of the role of First Lady: "I think it's an important role for the First Lady to look after the President's health and well-being. And if that interferes with other plans, so be it.... The First Lady is, after all, a wife." Richard E. Neustadt rated her performance highly in this regard, marking her efforts as needed support for a president, the kind of personal backup unlikely to come from others.

Hillary Clinton provides another starkly different portrayal—one of a political and policy activist First Lady. In entering the White House, her husband promised "two for the price of one." Mrs. Clinton's NFLL perspective varied substantially from those of Eleanor Roosevelt and Nancy Reagan: "The American people have made the role of First Lady one of the most important jobs in the country." She provided a representative cast to the position—that of reflecting the wishes of the American people. And she thereby elevated its importance.

In January 1993, President Clinton appointed his wife to head the Task Force on National Health Care Reform, directly involving her in policy planning and support on a high-priority issue. Thus from the start the First Lady was deeply involved in politics. Subsequently, she was involved in children's health insurance and women's rights issues. She traveled extensively, setting a record for the number of countries visited by a First Lady.

Ms. Clinton continued her political life beyond her years as First Lady. In 2000, she ran for and won the US Senate seat from New York and was reelected in 2006. In 2008 she sought the Democratic nomination for president, but lost narrowly to Barack Obama. President Obama appointed her secretary of state, in which post she served for four years. She again sought the Democratic nomination for president in 2015–16.

Eleanor Roosevelt and Hillary Clinton stand out among First Ladies as the most active in that role. In fact, it was said that Ms. Clinton was "channeling" Ms. Roosevelt. However, Ms. Roosevelt was much less directly involved than Hillary Clinton in the politics of issues in Washington and in campaigning for office. It is unclear how much Hillary Clinton's experiences will influence future First Ladies. Often her work invited criticism and conflict. At the very least, however, one may expect a greater range of service than serving as White House hostess.

Chief of state

Most nations have a chief of state, a person designated to play the role of ceremonial leader—the face to the world. Often these persons are called "presidents," with prime ministers serving as political leaders. Some nations have royal families, with the monarch serving as chief of state, as with Queen Elizabeth of Great Britain or King Felipe VI of Spain. Religious leaders too may perform that role, for example, Ayatollah Khamenei in Iran. The United States does not separate the ceremonial and political leadership posts. The president serves both as chief of state and chief executive.

The role of chief of state is multi-dimensional. In this role the president must stand above partisan politics as an institutional figure, one representing the whole nation. As chief of state the president may be seen throwing out the first ball of the baseball season, a tradition started by President William Howard Taft in 1910, or awarding medals recognizing valor in battle or outstanding achievement in a career. The annual message to Congress on the State of the Union is acknowledged as a constitutionally authorized ceremony, one in which the president plays chief of state and chief policy agenda setter. The president also leads the nation in grieving for the loss of life in national tragedies, for example, George W. Bush's appearances on the site of the 9/11 destruction of the World Trade Center or Obama's travel to view the devastation in the wake of Hurricane Sandy in New Jersey and New York.

In traveling outside the country, the president is viewed by foreign citizens as representing the United States, uncomplicated by the complexities of the separation of powers back home. Similarly, presidential communications at international conferences are interpreted as reflecting American views. Presidents also receive new ambassadors to the United States in symbolic recognition of national acceptance of their diplomatic positions. And presidents occasionally host state dinners at the White House for visiting heads of state, typically grand occasions receiving worldwide media coverage.

In fulfilling the role of chief of state, the president is aided by the Department of State's chief of protocol, with the rank of ambassador and assistant secretary of state. Responsible for diplomatic decorum and practices, this officer advises the president, manages the scheduling of visiting foreign dignitaries, and accompanies the president in an advisory capacity on official foreign travel. Often the job is very demanding, as, for example, when, in September 2015, Pope Francis and Chinese President Xi Jinping (receiving a state dinner) arrived in the same week, followed by a meeting between President Obama and Russian President Putin at the United Nations in New York the next Monday.

The presidential branch

White House staff efforts to connect with the permanent government so as to coordinate policy and politics inevitably replicate functions performed elsewhere. The EOP requires experienced and expert staff familiar with government programs, suggesting the need for low turnover. The WHO, as the organization tailored more to an individual president, will also need its team of policy and operational functionaries. As a lyric in *The Music Man* stated forcefully, they all "need to know the territory."

Institutionalization of this "help" to the president has produced what scholars refer to as a *presidential branch* operating to provide more control and greater coordination between the White House and the departments and agencies. What results is not exactly a chain of command, as in the military. Rather it provides a more coordinated and effective, though not formalized, structure of what has become a sizable presidential staff favoring the president's policy and political preferences.

The work by White House staff can lead to conflicts and interference with the efforts of the president's own appointees in the cabinet departments and other agencies, as well as the bureaucrats in those units. And, as with any expanding organization, competition may develop among staff for the boss's favor. George E. Reedy, who served President Lyndon Johnson as press secretary, likened White House staff machinations to "the life of the barnyard, as set forth so graphically in the study of the pecking order among chickens."

One need not accept Reedy's rather harsh and vivid portrayal to comprehend the hazards for presidents in ensuring that the presidential branch works for them and not simply to advance the ambitions of their staffs or get in the way of effective governance. It is unquestionably the case that working for the president can be an important credentialing experience, leading to other positions of status and financial reward if one moves to the private sector. In fact, Washington is teeming with former presidential staff appointees now lobbying for various interests. Thus presidents cannot always be assured the goals of staff will mesh with those set for the administration.

Other management problems within the presidential branch include staff members becoming public figures (something advised against in the 1937 report), preventing leaks as staff expands, maintaining personal loyalty among those less known to the president, and avoiding staff fatigue.

The latter point is less well recognized than the others. White House staff positions can easily become open-ended in two respects: working hours and job definition. Jeffrey H. Birnbaum, in his book *Madhouse*, an analysis of "the private turmoil of working for the president," states that working in the White House is for the young. The pace and lack of clear specification of responsibilities take their toll. As Birnbaum emphasizes, expectations of the president are greater than anyone can possibly meet, yet the staffs are responsible for meeting them.

Presidents and their advisers can study how it was done before. But no one president is like another, and much depends on the preferences, qualities, capabilities, resources, backgrounds, and goals that shape the style and approach of the new leader in town. Presidents are advised to "hit the ground running." Yet without having established reliable connections to the permanent government, a new president and staff may only be running in place.

White House operations do tend to improve with time. As it happens, however, just as the staff and major appointees are settling into governing routines, it is time for the president to seek reelection. Three things happen at that point: the inner circle becomes occupied with the campaign (staff are often added specifically for that purpose), those major appointees still serving think seriously about resigning their positions, and reelection itself alters how those in the permanent government view the White House—the so-called lame duck condition. Thus, presidents in their second term must make organizational adjustments just as their network of relationships has matured. To say the least, connecting to and leading the government are dynamic processes requiring patience and deftness.

Chapter 6
Presidents at work: making law and doing policy

Presidents are decision makers who work at a job structured by the tension between what is expected and what can be delivered. The strain derives mostly from the way the Founders sought to make a government that would work—but only interactively among its several parts. The Founders divided authority and constrained powers. Consequently, making decisions is typically a joint enterprise. Congress can pass bills, but the president signs them into law, or perhaps not. Presidents can negotiate treaties, but two-thirds of the Senate must approve, or perhaps not. The Supreme Court can negate a law, but Congress and the president can achieve their purposes by enacting a law that avoids the issue raised by the Court. I think the Founders would be pleased with how the separated system has developed, primarily because many of the same institutional issues debated in Philadelphia remain core topics today. In particular, this question remains open: How powerful should the president be?

Joint enterprise or no, presidents are held accountable for what happens in Washington. It is the president's job approval, now tested hundreds of times a year, receiving national public attention. Why? There is only one president at a time. Presidents are, effectively, the only nationally elected officials. They serve as the commanders in chief, a title surely conveying authority, and so they are expected to lead and achieve. No excuses, certainly not one stating: "But you don't understand; this is a joint enterprise."

Coincidentally, presidents are expected to observe the limits of their authority—to avoid abusing it, to acknowledge the legitimacy of the other branches, and to respect the right of the public to know the what and how of decision making. Is it fair to hold presidents accountable for what happens in a shared-powers government? I leave that to you to decide. It is, however, clear from history that they will be held accountable for the reasons stated, and therefore it comes with the job. Those who seek the presidency surely know this in advance. Those who occupy the White House experience their preeminence in responsibility firsthand. President Truman stated it bluntly and tersely: "The buck stops here."

A look inside the president's working world reveals the nature of making decisions and the president's roles and functions in the processes involved. Interdependency is a major feature of an interlocking separation-of-powers system, with each branch exercising authority that enables or thwarts the work of the others.

Lawmaking and its execution provide examples of substantive interdependency. Presidents designate agendas and propose what should be done. Congresses represent constituency interests in legislating from this agenda. The bureaucracy implements the laws passed by congresses and signed by presidents. The courts judge challenges to laws and how these laws are implemented. It is true that the institutions share and compete for powers, but seldom will the work of one branch be mistaken for the work of another. Should there be encroachment, such meddling will likely be strongly criticized, perhaps even challenged in the courts.

Split-party governments in recent decades, accompanied by narrow margins for political parties, have encouraged presidents to work independently on major issues. Frustrated by lack of support or stalemate in Congress, Presidents George W. Bush on war making and intelligence gathering and Obama on health care, environmental, and immigration issues tested their powers to act solely within the executive. In some cases the Supreme Court ruled they could not do so. Typically, however, court procedures were lengthy, often permitting the president's decisions to stand for months or even years.

Given their national and international exposure, presidents typically need to think prospectively, weighing the effects of initiatives and decisions on their capacities to govern in the future. George W. Bush was quoted as saying: "I think my job is to stay ahead of the moment. A president . . . can get so bogged down in the moment that you're unable to be the strategic thinker that you're supposed to be." Presidential scholar Richard E. Neustadt had a more nuanced analysis. He concluded that presidents who think politically guide themselves into protecting their influence for making future choices. For example, in 1994 Clinton reduced his options in regard to national health care proposals when he threatened to veto a version not to his liking. Speaking before Congress in the State of the Union message, Clinton made his arguments for a health care plan. Then he waved his pen in the air and warned of a veto. The former president acknowledged the mistake in his memoirs:

> I thought my argument was effective except for one thing: at the end . . . I held up a pen and said I would use it to veto any bill that didn't guarantee health insurance to all Americans. . . . It was an unnecessary red flag to my opponents in Congress. Politics is about compromise and people expect Presidents to win, not posture for them.

In the end, the plan failed in both houses of a Democratic Congress.

President Obama made the "deadline" error very early in his administration. Following his inauguration he issued an executive order to close Guantanamo Bay prison in Cuba within a year. He held a public signing ceremony for the order. The decision met with opposition both among voters and on Capitol Hill. Not only did the government miss the deadline but the prison remained open for years after his order. Seemingly, neither the president nor his staff had thought ahead to possible failure to meet the deadline, thus ignoring Neustadt's advice to protect one's influence in making future choices.

Working with Congress

Presidents interact with countless officials and groups in their manifold formal and informal roles, for example, as diplomats with foreign nations, as party leaders with politicians, as managers with agency personnel, as educators with the public, as grievers with those experiencing tragedies, and as commanders with the armed forces. Among the most important and perpetual relationships, however, are those between the president and members of Congress. The budget process alone ensures that the president will pay close attention to Capitol Hill. "No Money shall be drawn from the Treasury but in Consequence of Appropriations made by Law" (Art. I, Sec. 9). Put simply: Lacking appropriations by Congress, the government is stymied, constitutionally unable to draw funds from the Treasury, as happened in 1995 and 2013 when Presidents Clinton and Obama were at loggerheads with a split-party Congress over the budget.

Presidents differ in their working relationships with Congress. Their political and governmental backgrounds largely explain this variation. A few examples illustrate the differences among recent presidents. Lyndon Johnson served in the House (twelve years) and Senate (twelve years, ten as a leader). He was effectively *majority leader as president*. As Ralph K. Huitt, who worked for Johnson, observed: "He learned early and never forgot the basic skill of the politician, the ability to divide any number by two and add one." As was the case when he was in Congress, Johnson as president was a master builder of majorities on Capitol Hill in support of his Great Society programs.

Richard Nixon had also served in Congress but not as a leader and for six, not twenty-four, years. His interest and expertise were in foreign policy. He was *foreign minister as president*, preferring to work on national security and international relations issues. As such, he did not want frequent contact with members of Congress, whose primary interests tend to be in domestic issues. A House Republican was quoted as saying: "I pretty well concluded that there was almost no way to contact him except if you had a personal relationship."

Jimmy Carter likewise did not invite frequent or close contact with members of Congress. The reasons were different, however, again related to his background. Elected as a post-Watergate president, Carter was skeptical of the politics of compromise that dominated Congress. He was the *political layman as president*. Ignoring his narrow win in 1976, it was his view that the president represents all the people and has resources to develop comprehensive programs. He stressed the importance of doing the right thing over bargaining.

Reagan, Clinton, and George W. Bush were, like Carter, governors before serving as presidents. Accordingly they brought variations of an executive orientation to their work with Congress. True to his profession in private life, Reagan was an *actor as president*. His view of his status was best summarized by the subtitle of Lou Cannon's book: *President Reagan: The Role of a Lifetime*. Unlike Carter, Reagan was not in the least opposed to compromise, which fit his understanding of the role to be played by the president. He viewed his responsibilities as those of designating and defining a limited agenda, delegating responsibility to staff for working out details, agreeing to an acceptable compromise, and declaring victory. In Reagan's political theater, he accepted Clinton's view that "people expect presidents to win."

Clinton was a *campaigner as president*. Few presidents in history had as much experience in running for office—for the House of Representatives, for attorney general and six times for governor in Arkansas, and twice for president. He continued to sell his programs even after winning the presidency. Each State of the Union message was followed by travel to bolster public support for his proposals.

George W. Bush adopted Clinton's practice of campaigning for policy as well as election. In fact, Bush topped Clinton's record-setting travel, prompting one scholar to dub Bush a campaigner president. Clinton's and Bush's styles and purposes differed, however. Bush's way of working was that of a *pure executive as president*. As the most separationist of presidents, Bush believed he and Congress practiced distinct functions. He viewed his job as designating the issues and offering proposals to Congress; he saw it much less as working, Johnson-like, to build majorities on Capitol Hill. His campaigning was primarily to convince the public he had the right priorities and the most effective plans. As with Nixon, he also demonstrated an expansive interpretation of his powers in regard to national security and intelligence-gathering issues.

Barack Obama was among the least prepared by experience to serve as president. He lacked background as an executive and working time in Washington. He served three terms as an Illinois state senator and a partial term as a US senator. Prior to elective office, he taught constitutional law and was a community activist. His role evolved into a *transformationalist president*. Bolstered initially by a Democratic Congress, Obama offered an ambitious agenda for change, expecting the Democratic Congress to design and enact legislation on health care, financial control, energy, climate change, and economic stimulation. Narrow partisan passage of the Affordable Care Act was a notable achievement. Obama was even more active in campaigning for proposals than Clinton and George W. Bush. In 2010, Republicans recaptured

8. President George W. Bush on the road, campaigning for public support of his agenda.

majority status in the House of Representatives, thereby positioning themselves to block many subsequent reform proposals. Republicans took back the Senate as well in 2014.

Other post–World War II presidents show equally diverse manners of dealing with Congress: Eisenhower—military commander; Kennedy—junior senator; Ford—minority leader; George H. W. Bush—career diplomat. Presidents approach the job with individual perspectives that help shape their responses to the issues they encounter and to the events generating those issues.

Policy substance

Presidents make many types of decisions in varieties of settings. Their policy world is fast paced and complex. They deal in policy substance and its phases and processes. Much of what happens is routine, essentially handled by the bureaucrats, appointed political executives and their aides, and policy specialists, presumably all attentive to presidential priorities. Ultimately, however, presidents are held responsible because they have the authority to say yes, no, or try again.

Substance refers to the "what" of policy, that is, the meat of a proposal. Most substantive issues fit within two broad categories: domestic and foreign. The two sets have interactive effects. Energy supply and demand is a fine example of a domestic issue with significant impact on foreign policy. Terrorism brings an international issue home in the form of homeland security threats. Many issues are not only interactive substantively

Table 6.1 Important Enactments, Clinton–Bush–Obama Presidencies (1993–2014)

Clinton (1993–2001)	
Same Party	**Split Party**
103rd Congress = 11 enactments	104th Congress = 15 enactments
	105th Congress = 9 enactments
	106th Congress = 6 enactments
Bush (2001–2009)	
Same Party	**Split Party**
107th Congress = 1 enactment*	107th Congress = 16 enactments
108th Congress = 10 enactments	
109th Congress = 14 enactments	110th Congress = 13 enactments
Obama (2009–2015)	
Same Party	**Split Party**
111th Congress = 16 enactments	112th Congress = 7 enactments
	113th Congress = 10 enactments

* For the first five months, Republicans had House and Senate majorities.

Source: Compiled from David R. Mayhew, *Divided We Govern: Party Control, Lawmaking, and Investigations, 1946–2002* (New Haven, CT: Yale University Press, 2005), 208–13, and http://pantheon.yale.edu/~dmayhew.

between their domestic and foreign dimensions but are, as well, institutionally diverse, with Congress more attuned to domestic matters, the executive to foreign aspects.

Major legislation on highly diverse policy issues was enacted during the Clinton, George W. Bush, and Obama presidencies. A large number became law in split-party government. Why choose these presidencies for illustrative purposes, apart from their currency? Because they exhibit the challenges for the White House in managing policy substance at a time of narrow-margin politics. Notably relevant are the growing tensions between the two competing branches. These fractures often encourage the president to pursue means for resolving substantive issues within the executive branch, perhaps with executive orders or agency rule making. Recall the point made earlier that presidents may, given close two-party margins or opposite party congressional majorities, think more favorably of Alexander Hamilton's presidential presidency, less so of James Madison's separated presidency. Such independent action has consequences, eliciting as it does the specter of defying the protections of the separation of powers, most notably the benefits of the full range of the representational mix in Congress.

What explains the special nature of these three presidencies? They are historic—the first cases of three successive two-term administrations since Jefferson-Madison-Monroe (1801–25). In contrast with their predecessors, however, Clinton-George W. Bush-Obama entered the White House with more limited political capital, as a set with the lowest popular vote margins in the post–World War II era. Clinton won the popular vote with a plurality in a three-candidate race. George W. Bush lost the popular vote to Gore and barely won the electoral vote following a recount in Florida. Obama won more handily, but a 53 percent popular vote was still not approaching the proportions of postwar landslide victors such as Eisenhower, Johnson, Nixon, and Reagan.

Reelection for each of the three was a marginal improvement—still not a majority popular vote, but a comfortable electoral count, for Clinton; very narrow popular and electoral votes for George W. Bush; and a dip in popular vote for Obama. Furthermore, Clinton and Obama returned with Republicans in Congress also winning—both houses for Clinton, the House of Representatives for Obama.

Not one of these three presidents served through the two terms with his party in control of Congress. Each started that way, but it did not last. In fact, there were nine combinations of party splits in their twenty-four years in the White House. There were twice as many years with split-party control (one house or both) than of single-party control. Clinton had the longest period with the same party division—six years—but it was with a Republican Congress.

To say the least, such fluctuation in political party status in the national government required each president to be flexible and adaptable in managing policy substance. So what happened during these presidencies? Were important laws passed and signed by the president? Were presidents able to build majorities for their priorities? How did they manage unanticipated events?

Expectations were high for the Clinton presidency in spite of his plurality popular vote. The Democrats had won the presidency and majorities on Capitol Hill for the first time in twelve years. The president came well prepared with policy proposals. His "Putting People First" campaign document offered a national economic strategy ("the economy, stupid") with thirty-five proposals. Following were thirty-one issue sets accompanied by 577 proposals. Truly, no past president had ever opened with a more expansive, detailed, or ambitious substantive agenda.

The Democratic 103rd Congress passed eleven major bills. Most notable were a deficit reduction package, the North American Free Trade Agreement (NAFTA), Americorps, the Brady gun control law, and an omnibus crime law. What did not pass, or even come to a vote in either chamber, was the president's priority social welfare proposal: a national health care program.

Republicans won a huge victory in the 1994 midterm election, winning both houses. The political landscape was transformed. A dramatic change in policy substance occurred, with shifts to deregulation, reorganization, spending cuts, and reforms. The most significant major act was welfare reform, a Republican priority opposed by many Democrats but signed by Clinton after two vetoes.

The most notable face-off in the 104th Congress was budgetary. Republican Speaker of the House Newt Gingrich's confrontations with President Clinton in 1995 led twice to partial shutdowns of the federal government before Gingrich acquiesced and supported passing a budget. Clinton's win was notable in restoring his status in national politics following the disastrous 1994 midterm election defeat. But he was leading on Republican turf, even declaring at one point: "The era of big government is over."

Clinton's reelection in 1996 was accompanied by a return of the Republican Congress. A centrist to center-right agenda prevailed, initially featuring bipartisan cooperation with congressional Republicans. The most important substantive product was a balanced budget agreement incorporating children's health benefits and tax cuts. This achievement encouraged Clinton to resume leadership of the agenda in his 1998 State of the Union message. However, the revelation of the Monica Lewinsky indiscretion disrupted the president's plan. Investigation and impeachment proceedings preoccupied Washington through 1998 and into 1999.

George W. Bush's transition to the White House in 2000–01 was truncated by the Florida recount, extending to December and finally halted by the US Supreme Court decision in *Bush v. Gore*.

Republicans had a net loss of seats in the House of Representatives but remained in the majority. The Senate was tied, dependent on Vice President Cheney's vote for Republicans to organize the chamber. It was not an auspicious start.

Bush lacked an agenda document to match that offered post-election by the Clinton team. However, Bush started with items believed to attract bipartisan support: tax cuts and education reform ("No Child Left Behind"). The fragile Republican control of the Senate broke in favor of the Democrats when James Jeffords (R-Vermont) left his party to become an independent, voting with the Democrats for organizational purposes. Bush's tax cuts were enacted but little else of importance followed during the summer given Democrats'control of the Senate agenda.

On September 11, 2001, the national agenda changed with the terrorist attacks on the World Trade Center in New York City and the Pentagon in Washington. Consequently, a major substantive agenda replaced those of the president and Senate Democrats. Bush's job approval ratings skyrocketed to record levels. The president's political stock increased dramatically and important enactments tumbled out of Washington, the most numerous for any Congress in the Clinton to Obama era.

Just one of the important enactments, tax cuts, was passed before 9/11. One other, education reform, was enacted subsequently on a bipartisan vote. One of the five actions in 2001 was a congressional resolution authorizing the president to use force against those involved in terrorist acts against the United States. The other four were designed to strengthen security at home. Cross-party support in both chambers characterized each enactment.

Security and war continued to dominate policy substance in 2002. Of the ten important enactments, five were directly classified as such, including a use of force resolution against Iraq, the controversial creation of a Department of Homeland Security, and creation of a commission to study 9/11.

The 2002 midterm election bolstered Bush's political status. Republicans had net increases in both the House and Senate, thus giving the president's party majorities in both chambers. These positive shifts provided Bush with an opportunity to return to a more traditional Republican agenda—for example, tax cuts, limits on abortion, defense funding increases, corporate tax restructuring, and reorganizations. A prescription drug benefit and AIDS funding in Africa were also enacted.

On reelection in 2004, Bush vowed to use what he interpreted as an endorsement to support an ambitious agenda. His priority issue was Social Security reform. He campaigned hard for his proposals outside Washington, faring no better than Clinton had done with health care. Bush had to work as hard for Republican votes as those of Democrats. Once again, entitlement reform was judged by most members of Congress to threaten constituent clienteles. Bush's plan did not make it to the floor in either chamber.

In late August 2005, yet another agenda-altering event occurred: a Category 5 hurricane hit the Gulf Coast, with devastating effects in New Orleans. Bush was heavily criticized for the poor federal government response. Meanwhile the Iraq war was not going well and President Bush's job approval rating was declining sharply from the record heights following 9/11. The 2006 midterm election brought House and Senate Democratic majorities back to Capitol Hill. Bush set in place a surge of troops in Iraq in 2007, with positive results in the war but little improvement in the president's standing.

As a final blow, the economy began slipping, requiring another agenda shift. During the fall election, economic woes culminated in a financial sector breakdown which brought the two presidential candidates to the White House for a conference with the president and congressional leaders.

The national government in 2007–08 was in transition. Democrats had moved to leadership positions on Capitol Hill and the president's status deteriorated almost to custodial service. The more serious substantive action came in 2008, associated with the worsening of the economy. Three of the eight important enactments dealt with this issue, concluding with the passage of a $700 billion bailout of the financial sector and tax breaks in October. It was a remarkable piece of bipartisan legislation just prior to election day, signifying the policy priorities for the new administration.

Barack Obama entered the White House with a comfortable but not overwhelming election victory. He had an ambitious substantive agenda but needed first to act on the present economic crisis. To his advantage, the Democratic Congress returned with increased majorities in both houses. The additional Senate number brought Democrats very close to the sixty votes required to thwart a filibuster.

The first important enactment was not long in coming. House and Senate Democrats worked on an economic stimulus bill during the lame-duck Congress in 2008 so as to have it ready when Obama was inaugurated. President Obama signed a nearly $800 billion dollar package of grants, investments, tax cuts, and credits on February 17, 2009, less than a month after he was sworn in. From that point forward, major legislative actions flowed from Congress expanding existing federal programs and regulations, creating new initiatives, and preparing the groundwork for national health care, energy proposals, and financial sector regulations. It was like the days of old for Democrats—the FDR and Lyndon Johnson eras.

The following year was even more productive. Congressional Democrats enacted the Affordable Care Act (Obamacare) and the

Wall Street Reform and Consumer Protection Act (Dodd-Frank), both transformative, historic enactments. Neither gained support from the minority Republicans. However encouraging this production was to the White House, the 2010 midterm elections that followed dramatically altered the prospects for more. House Republicans won a majority with a net gain of sixty-three seats, one of the largest swings in decades. Senate Republicans had a net gain of six seats but Democrats narrowly retained their majority in that chamber.

With a majority of 242 to 193 in the House, Republicans were in a position to block the president's agenda. Accordingly, the Democrats moved some of the president's priorities during a lame-duck congressional session before the newly elected Republicans could be sworn in. One bipartisan action was an extension of Bush's tax cuts for an additional two years.

Much like the Clinton years, the eagerness and excitement of productive policy substance in the first two years of the Obama presidency were absent in 2011–12. So too was the agenda. The new focus was on making deals for raising the debt ceiling, cutting spending, and raising taxes, along with two trade agreements. The president was boxed in by the House Republicans and they were, in turn, boxed in by the Senate Democrats. And the 2012 presidential election was upcoming. A sour mood returned to Washington—just seven important laws were passed in the 113th Congress.

President Obama won reelection by a smaller popular and electoral vote than in 2008, which was unusual historically. Each party retained its majority—Democrats in the Senate; Republicans in the House. Virtually, therefore, Washington politics remained frozen in place. However, as with George W. Bush in 2005, Obama pressed forward aggressively with an active agenda and positive attitude but little success.

When the 113th Congress adjourned, few knew what to make of its product. Important enactments were limited to a highly disparate collection of items with little coherence or identity as an Obama program. The president relied on executive orders and agency rulings for policy decisions on health care, immigration, environmental standards, and financial sector revisions.

The 2014 midterm election was a substantial defeat for Democrats. Republicans had a net gain of nine Senate seats for a majority of fifty-four and a net gain of thirteen House seats to reach their largest majority in recent decades. The decline in numbers for congressional Democrats over the six years of the Obama presidency seriously hindered White House management of policy substance.

The Clinton-Bush-Obama period illustrates the vagaries of policy substance in a separated powers system. The White House is typically thought of as the standard source of an agenda, but it may lose its hold on setting priorities. Unexpected events, political shifts, loss of standing, blockages, economic downsweeps, even personal behavior can alter what is worked on and whether or not the White House wins.

The variations in political party control of the elected branches between 1993 and 2015 is surely allowable and predictable in a government of separated elections. It represents how voters made their choices, essentially letting both parties win. What the period demonstrates, however, is potentially a *deformation* of separated system politics and institutional interactions, with important effects on policy substance.

When presidents test the limits of executive powers with orders, rule making, or failures to enforce laws rather than relying on Congress to legislate changes, such decisions may well be challenged in the federal courts. The consequence is lawmaking by the executive, overseen by the courts. Congress is left out unless directed to be involved by court direction. Furthermore, drawing the courts into defining the validity of presidential actions takes time, during which potentially unconstitutional policy may well be implemented. Should such presidential-federal court interaction become regularized, it would be deformative of the separation of powers by leaving out Congress.

Foreign policy discretion

The president's discretionary powers in foreign and national security policy are substantial and well illustrated by the Clinton-Bush-Obama presidencies. These powers may become the subject of controversy, often inviting congressional investigations and oversight largely because Congress had little or no role in the initiatives taken by the president.

Outstanding examples of discretionary actions during the Clinton presidency include both military action and peace initiatives. Congress was not asked to authorize any of the US bombing raids in Serbia or Iraq. Clinton also sponsored peace initiatives as largely executive actions. In November 1995, the Dayton Peace Accords ended the conflict in Bosnia. In July 2000, Clinton hosted a summit at Camp David to resolve issues between the Israeli government and the Palestinian Authority.

Likewise, the second Bush presidency provides countless examples of the president making military and diplomatic commitments with little or no direct involvement of Congress. Even the congressional 2001 Use of Force Resolution (Afghanistan) and 2002 Iraq resolutions largely left open the timing, rationale, and form of military action. Much of the controversy developing over treatment of prisoners resulted from executive and military decisions regarding the incarceration of terrorists, decisions that in the earliest stages were not subject to the kind of close scrutiny of open congressional hearings. President Bush was initially reluctant to be involved in resolving Israeli-Palestinian issues.

Later, however, his administration became heavily committed with the Road Map to Peace initiative in May 2003.

Obama did not seek congressional authorization for using military force in Libya, acting in conjunction with NATO forces. Nor did he seek approval for his reduction of forces in Iraq when senators on the Armed Services Committee warned of the effects. Obama's most controversial diplomatic effort, however, was conducting negotiations with Iran regarding sanctions and nuclear power. Supporters of Israel were notably troubled.

When purely executive actions produce positive results, support follows in Congress. Where serious problems develop or the resolution of an issue takes longer than expected (as with the Vietnam War, the Iraq insurgency, or the rise of the Islamic State), Congress vigorously exercises its oversight role with investigations and threatened limitations on presidential discretion. Congress is constrained if military action is under way. It has the power of the purse, but members are reluctant to deny funds to the troops. It is also the case in modern warfare that a military mission may have been completed by the time Congress acts. The problem is somewhat different in regard to diplomacy. Treaties require Senate approval (two-thirds of those present) and financial commitments need congressional authorization and appropriation. Presidents can avoid seeking Senate approval by negotiating an "agreement" rather than a treaty, as with the nuclear agreement with Iran in 2015. In any event, the executive decides where, when, and what to negotiate. Congress does not have a separate diplomatic corps. In foreign policy, presidents exercise their greatest influence, whether Congress approves or not.

Policy types

The president's role also differs by the type of policy under consideration. Most policy proposals fall into four broad categories: fresh initiatives, incremental adjustments to existing programs, major overhauls of programs on the books, and crisis response. Different types of policies lend themselves to more or less empowerment for the president.

Fresh initiatives are most likely to come from the executive and are often proposed when a new president takes office. For example, in his first year Clinton successfully proposed an Americorps to encourage young people to do volunteer work in the community in exchange for educational support. George W. Bush favored a faith-based initiative for spurring community-level aid to the disadvantaged. Congress did not enact the proposed legislation, so Bush issued an executive order initiating certain aspects of the proposal. Obama championed national health insurance with an individual mandate to sign up or be fined. His proposal passed narrowly with Democratic votes only—not recommended for such a mega-program.

Fresh programs are more difficult to enact than in the past, largely because of the cost of those put on the books in the FDR through the Johnson presidencies. Entitlement programs such as Social Security, Medicare, and Medicaid, federal aid to education, home loan guarantees, food stamps, and other welfare benefits, along with national defense, have left little room in the budget for new initiatives. Therefore, new programs typically must include innovative financing, sometimes with proposals to reduce expenditures elsewhere, referred to as "pay-go."

Incrementalism characterizes most existing government programs for several reasons: more persons are covered by the benefits as the population grows and ages, costs of living rise, and organized groups make claims. For example, the many programs providing benefits for senior citizens have grown in size as people live longer, have more health problems, and are represented by politically active groups, notably the American Association of Retired Persons (AARP).

9. President Johnson signs the Medical Care for the Aged Act of 1965, a Great Society program, in the presence of former President Harry S. Truman, who first proposed a health plan in 1945.

The politics of incrementalism are predictable. Once in place, entitlement programs, such as Social Security and Medicare, grow automatically. The only way to curb spending is to change eligibility, a move most presidents and members of Congress are cautious in proposing. As the agenda designators, presidents learn that any such proposals, even for needed reforms, can ignite political firestorms on Capitol Hill and among beneficiaries. Presidents thus carefully calculate the political risks involved in proposing major changes.

Presidents occasionally propose major overhauls of existing programs in spite of the potential costs for taking a chance. There comes a time when most government programs are subject to serious review and change. That time will occur in the decades following the enactment of large-scale programs like those of Franklin Roosevelt's New Deal and Johnson's Great Society. Thus it is not surprising in recent years to find that the executive branch proposals to Congress have "reform" in their titles: for example, Social Security and welfare reform, Medicare reform, farm subsidy reform, public housing reform. Most often the changes proposed are refinements, but occasionally they are root-and-branch recastings, as with welfare reform in 1996 or the Affordable Care Act in 2010, and these generate intense controversy.

The reforms proposed for Social Security are at a very high risk, as was confirmed for Bush in 2005 when he supported private accounts as an option for a portion of payroll taxes paid. His plan did not get beyond the committee stage in either house of Congress. Immigration reform is also a political minefield, again as experienced by Bush in 2006. Faced with stalemate in Congress on the issue, Obama decided to act by executive order in 2015, a move inviting challenges in the federal courts as exceeding his constitutional authority.

It was long thought that welfare reform carried many of the same political risks as immigration and Social Security. President Clinton made it a priority in his first term, an unusual step for a Democrat. Yet he placed it second to health care reform. Meanwhile, congressional Republicans agreed with the welfare reform priority. When they gained majorities in the House and Senate in 1994, they took the initiative in fashioning a plan. President Clinton twice vetoed the bill but signed it when the Republican Congress passed it a third time. Many Democrats were critical of Clinton's action, and some in his own administration resigned.

The risks for Clinton in these two cases—national health care and welfare reform—were multiple and sequential. He proposed taking on two major reforms, failed utterly in the first, then lost the initiative for the second, welfare reform, to the Republicans. Finally signing the Republican bill the third time around invited criticism from his own party. There are few better cases of the hazards of proposing root-and-branch reforms.

Presidents are frequently rated by how well they respond to crises. By definition, such events interfere with the regular order. Yet their effects may be widespread, and the public's expectations are that response will come immediately from the executive, led and directed by the president. Congress will participate but typically following the lead of the commander in chief.

One of the most dramatic examples of crisis response were George W. Bush's decisions following the terrorist attacks on September 11, 2001, which reoriented his agenda and elicited bipartisan support for forceful action.

In striking contrast, support for the president was substantially less forthcoming for the war in Iraq, both initially and even more with continued insurgent attacks following the completion of full-scale military action. The difference? The president had difficulty persuading his critics and, eventually, many in the public that Saddam Hussein's rule in Iraq represented a crisis or that it was directly related to the war on terrorism. These doubts were reinforced when no weapons of mass destruction were found in Iraq. In other words, many in Congress and the public at large did not consider the war in Iraq to be appropriate crisis response.

The Katrina hurricane was another example of crisis response, one substantially less favorable to Bush's leadership than 9/11. No one doubted that Katrina was a crisis or that response was required by the national government. But the effects were regional, not national, and the offender was Mother Nature, not terrorists. True, 9/11 was also localized, but the threat was pervasive.

In the case of Katrina, coordination among federal, state, and local governments was inadequate to manage an exceptional natural disaster. The president was bound to bear the responsibility as the chief of the branch that was expected to react effectively. The Katrina disaster is a prime example of presidential responsibility regardless of whether public expectations are realistic about the capacity of the president or the government to cope. It simply goes with the job of being at the top. No excuses.

Policy process

The process by which policy is set in place and implemented can be broken down into several phases or functions: problem definition, agenda designation, option formulation, and program legitimation, implementation, and evaluation. The president and his aides play different roles in each of these phases.

Problem definition starts it all. What requires the attention of the national government and why? There are, at minimum, two dimensions to consider: the broad issue (e.g., terrorism) and the specific problems (e.g., homeland security, identifying and capturing or eradicating the terrorists, managing the social and economic effects). Presidents ordinarily play a key role in identifying and articulating the issues and defining the problems to be resolved. They are in a strong position to direct public attention to an issue.

Yet presidents do not have the last word. What requires attention and why is often the subject of debate in Congress and the media, even when there is broad agreement on the seriousness of the issue. For example, in a post-9/11 America, immigration was generally acknowledged to be a vital issue. But some policymakers defined the problem as failure to control the borders and enforce existing laws; others emphasized the need to cope with millions of undocumented immigrants who have become a significant force in the American economy as a source of labor.

Agenda designation is essentially a priority-setting exercise. It is a supremely political act, and presidents have significant constitutional, institutional, and electoral advantages for specifying priorities. They deliver the State of the Union message, they are served by an elaborate bureaucracy supplying detailed justifications for priorities, and they work closely with budget planners who know the country's fiscal condition and the effects of addressing the proposed priorities.

Presidents differ in the extent to which they capitalize on these advantages. Determinants include the president's philosophy of governing (more activist or more passive), the nature and number of major issues, and the strength of the opposition party. For example, Eisenhower was not a strong policy activist; he served during relatively calm times, with few major issues; and Democrats had majorities in both houses of Congress during six of his eight years as president. By contrast, Johnson brought an expansionist outlook to his presidency, he had to manage an increasingly unpopular war in Vietnam, and his party had huge congressional majorities.

As expected, given the three determinants (philosophy, issues, and strength of the opposition), there are several combinations among the post–World War II presidents. Reagan had a philosophy of limited government, seeking to reduce taxes and bureaucracy; he served during a period of relative calm; and he had the surprise advantage of a Republican Senate for six of his eight years in office. His agenda dominated policy politics during his first years in office, and his legislative success in cutting taxes influenced the agendas of presidents to follow.

A president with mild public support can expect others to assume the role of agenda designator. House Speakers James Wright (D-Texas) and Newt Gingrich (R-Georgia) were active agenda-setters with the decline in political capital of George H. W. Bush and Clinton in 1989 and 1995, respectively. Obama faced a reconfigured power network for agenda designation following his first and second midterm elections after the takeover by Republicans of the House in 2011 and of the Senate in 2015.

Option formulation is also a natural function of the executive, due primarily to the expertise represented in the bureaucracy and its hierarchical structure. Presidents and their staffs make promises in campaigns and in response to issues during their service in the White House. Usually these pledges lack a detailed plan. Rather they require development by specialists within the relevant cabinet department or agency. Likewise, congressional committee staffs, often working with the personal staffs of the members, prepare modifications or alternatives.

Rarely can presidents expect Congress to endorse their options in full, even when their party has large majorities in that branch. Johnson's 1965 Medicare proposal was modified substantially by the Democratic chair of the House Committee on Ways and Means, Wilbur Mills (D-Arkansas), working with John Byrnes (R-Wisconsin), ranking Republican on the committee. Staying with a health care example, Clinton had his proposal for national reform rejected in both houses in spite of Democratic majorities. Still, for the major issues, it is typically the president who says: "Let's start here with this."

Legitimation is the process by which an option, usually a compromise, is approved. Mostly this is a legislative function, though presidents and their staffs are actively involved as bills move forward. They garner majority support through a sequence of stages within committees, the House and Senate chambers, and possibly conferences between the two chambers. This process may take months, even years. It is not uncommon with certain controversial proposals for Congress to repeat the stages several times before attaining agreements in all of the venues required for final passage. Because of the filibuster procedure in the Senate, it may require a supermajority (sixty members) even to debate a bill in that chamber. And by constitutional provision, a two-thirds Senate majority is required for approval of treaties and a two-thirds majority in both chambers for a constitutional amendment or to override a presidential veto.

Presidents, their aides, and department and agency personnel are typically active in this majority-building enterprise—sometimes in support, other times in opposition. A change in presidents, which ordinarily means a change in party, can mean a reversal in White House support or opposition. Ultimately the president has the constitutional authority to sign or veto a bill, or to let it become law without his signature after a ten-day period, Sundays excluded (unless Congress has adjourned, in which case it will not become law (Art. I, Sec. 7). Presidents frequently use this vital authority of saying "yes" or "no" to influence lawmaking during the several stages of majority building—for example, by threatening to veto a bill unless changes are made or withdrawing support, with the potential effect of changing votes.

There is a tendency in the media to keep score in lawmaking by counting the bills passed and signed into law in a session of Congress. But progress may be slow on major national issues because difficult differences have to be resolved. For example, it took some thirty years for the federal government to enact an aid to education program, long an exclusive province of state and local governments. Racial, religious, and federalism issues had to be resolved before a bill could finally gain majority support in both houses. Bills would pass in the House, only then to be filibustered by southern Democrats in the Senate. The Elementary and Secondary Education Act eventually passed in 1965 as part of Johnson's Great Society program.

Crisis can often speed up the legitimation process. Following 9/11, Congress passed the USA Patriot Act, a sweeping measure to provide the attorney general with the authority to gather intelligence on terrorists (through wiretaps, searches, detention, and other means of surveillance). Committee hearings and votes were bypassed in the Senate, and the Speaker intervened in the House to send a bill favored by the administration to the floor. The final bill passed overwhelmingly in both houses. Four years later, a reauthorization of the Patriot Act required months to pass.

Implementation is fundamentally a bureaucratic function, for which the president as chief executive will be held responsible. Lawmakers will typically provide directions on how and where programs are to be implemented. But bureaucrats are in charge of the applications, often with substantial discretion, depending on how much Congress instructs them. State and local governments often play a major role in implementing domestic programs, an additional complication in designating responsibility.

Large-scale programs representing new ventures, reorganizations, or major shifts in policy may take years to implement effectively. Medicare and Medicaid, enacted in 1965, are prime examples of substantial national government interventions into a multi-faceted, semipublic health care system. What began as relatively modest programs in the 1960s now are measured in hundreds of billions of dollars. In 2004, a prescription drug benefit was added, again accompanied in the early months by serious implementation difficulties.

Implementation of a different sort characterizes the federal government's response to calamities. Disaster relief programs have been expanded in recent decades. Almost by definition, however, it is hard to prepare for the unanticipated. Hurricane Katrina along the Gulf Coast in 2005 was such an event, arguably the greatest natural disaster ever to occur in the United States. Government response was judged to be inadequate for many reasons: the magnitude of the disaster, the coincidence of crisis response agencies undergoing major reorganizations at the time at all three levels of government, breakdown of communications and law enforcement, lack of coordination among state and local agencies, and uncertainties about who was in charge of what. Yet the person responsible for these and other failings was judged to be President Bush, an opinion held by most officials, the general public, and, ultimately, the president himself. The Katrina experience is a classic case of presidential accountability regardless of the circumstances. To a lesser extent, Obama experienced the same phenomenon with the Gulf of Mexico oil spill in April 2010. Each case illustrates the difficulty of making corrections mid-crisis or even learning how to avoid mistakes in the future.

Evaluation is the most diversified of the policy activities. Every branch is involved, along with private interests and organizations. The executive agencies charged with implementing programs typically must report to Congress on their progress in achieving goals. Inspectors general within these agencies have the responsibility of investigating fraud and misconduct. The Office of Management and Budget (OMB) evaluates programs on a continuous basis as it prepares budgets for future years.

Congressional committees have the responsibility of overseeing the implementation of programs. This oversight may occur in several forms: as a routine exercise in reauthorization and appropriation; through investigations, either by authorizing committees or the two oversight committees; or by the work of the Government Accountability Office (GAO). This office is a legislative branch agency specifically charged with providing Congress information about the effectiveness of government programs.

The judicial branch, too, may be asked to evaluate a program, testing it against a constitutional standard. Judicial review is not specifically assigned to the courts in Article III, but Chief Justice John Marshall argued successfully that it was emphatically implied in the Constitution, even in the oath taken by judges (*Marbury v. Madison*, 1803). However, the courts can exercise this authority only in response to a specific case.

Clientele groups, the media, think tanks, public interest or watchdog groups, task forces, and candidate organizations continuously evaluate programs on the books. The media play an especially important role for two reasons: their adversarial role in regard to politics and government, and the quantum increase in media outlets in recent decades. The first is explained by what is typically judged to be news—the negative more than the positive. The second represents a phase change in communication. Not only are there new forms, pervasive through the Internet and other electronic developments, but coverage is constant, "24/7," as the phrase has it.

One consequence of "all news, all the time" is White House adaptation by greatly expanding its communications operations. What was once a press secretary with a small staff is now several assistants to the president for communication-related functions, including speechwriting, community outreach, advance work for presidential travel, communications in regard to policy and planning, public liaison, and intergovernmental affairs.

Policy coordination: budgeting

For decades presidents dominated budgeting. The Budget and Accounting Act of 1921 authorized the president to prepare an annual budget, assisted by a Bureau of the Budget (originally a part of the Department of Treasury, later a part of the Executive Office of the President and still later renamed the Office of Management and Budget—OMB). The development of a budget in the executive is a multistage, year-long process of negotiation and refinement between the president and the departments and agencies, with OMB acting as the go-between. The result is then sent to Congress in a budget message. In the past, the revenue, appropriations, and authorizing committees in Congress relied almost entirely on the president's budget in doing their work, without ever considering the plan as a whole.

In 1974 that all changed when Congress created its own budget process with the passage of the Congressional Budget and Impoundment Control Act. The act created House and Senate budget committees, to be assisted by a Congressional Budget

Table 6.2 The Budget Process

Executive Phases

Preparation (March → February):	Year-long process of refinement and negotiation between the president, Office of Management and Budget (OMB), and agencies. OMB communicates presidential preferences and manages the details of adjusting agency requests to those preferences.
Submission (January → February):	President's budget message prepared and budget submitted to Congress.
Update (July):	President provides mid-session review.

Congressional Phases

Preparation (January → April):	Three-month-long process of review and breakdown of current and president's budget involving the Congressional Budget Office (CBO), the budget committees, and the revenue, appropriations, and authorizing committees.
Resolution (April):	Congress passes a concurrent budget resolution, with guidelines for committees.
Reconciliation (June → September):	Process of making adjustments to suit budget goals, again involving CBO, budget committees, and the revenue, appropriations, and authorizing committees.

Bureaucratic Phase

Execution (October 1→ September 30):	Agencies implement programs as authorized and appropriated by Congress.

Source: Compiled by the author from various sources.

Office (CBO), and formalized a process for regulating and monitoring the work of the other House and Senate committees. Deadlines were set to keep the process on schedule. Those deadlines have seldom been met.

Each branch prepares a budget, although the one in Congress is oriented to what has been prepared by the executive branch. The congressional process features negotiations between the budget committees in each house and the revenue, appropriations, and authorizing committees, with CBO providing expertise throughout. Not surprisingly, this process is tense and contentious, representing the interests served by the various committees as well as their protection of their jurisdictions. Yet in many ways it mirrors what happens in the executive between the agencies and the president and the OMB.

The period after 1974 has featured split-party government and narrow margins as political context for making budgets. Only Presidents Carter (four years, 1977–81), Clinton (1993–95), and Obama (2009–11) had comfortable party margins in Congress. Other presidents during this time (Ford, Reagan, George H. W. Bush, Clinton after 1994, George W. Bush, and Obama after 2010) either faced opposition party congresses (one house or both) or worked with very narrow party margins. While clashes were a certainty, presidents have the advantages of more detailed preparations, the veto threat, and a more coordinated approach to budgeting than Congress. Consequently, the executive typically wins more budget battles than they lose.

Results in the postwar era

Not all presidents are created equal. Likewise, not all presidents produce equally. Events appear to make the difference. Some presidents preside at turning points in history, others govern in periods of relative calm. The difference is not necessarily in the qualities or abilities of the incumbent. Crises are not selective. Rather, they test whoever happens to be in the White House at the time.

Post–World War II presidents at turning points include Truman, Johnson, Reagan, George W. Bush, and Obama. Truman had to manage the end of World War II, cope with its aftermath, and deal with the Korean conflict. Like Truman, Johnson served out the term of a popular president, Kennedy, whose assassination ensured support for his legacy. Johnson took charge of his predecessor's agenda and enacted the Great Society and civil rights reform programs that would dominate domestic policy from that time forward. Johnson did significantly less well with the developing crisis in Vietnam, where his record was as unimpressive as it was imposing on domestic issues.

Economic circumstances in 1980 provided Reagan with the support to reduce taxes and shift resources to defense. The effect of the first was to alter policy debate as deficits mounted; the second eventually contributed to the end of the Cold War and, later, the collapse of the Soviet Union. Few can doubt the significance of 9/11 for George W. Bush as a historic event of major impact on policy and politics. The war on terrorism, as extended by Bush to the war in Iraq, has had a profound effect on foreign and domestic politics. Terrorism remained a major focus for Obama as well. He also inherited a mega-recession and was responsible too for creating an event as turning point: national health insurance reform.

Events have also had an impact on the other postwar presidencies: Eisenhower, Nixon, Ford, Carter, George H.W. Bush, and Clinton. The terms in office of this second set of six presidents, however, have been characterized more by efforts to consolidate, strengthen, and reform policies and programs. Their presidencies were custodial, without implying anything disapproving about their personal abilities to cope with large-scale events had they occurred.

The remaining president in the postwar period, Kennedy, averted a potentially serious crisis with the threat posed by Soviet missiles in Cuba. Unquestionably his resolve in this matter was noteworthy and has been acknowledged as such by historians. The problem in classifying Kennedy lies in the brevity of his service.

Government has a momentum independent of who happens to be in the White House. Presidents at work aid in maintaining this momentum, facilitating ordinary change, and responding to unanticipated events. They are enablers of lawmaking, policymaking, and decision making. The executive branch is structured to promote these purposes in such a manner as to ensure congressional reliance on the president.

Perhaps most striking about a president's work is the need for agility and adaptability. Presidents are expected to produce comprehensive and coordinated programs, yet by its nature, a separation of powers government allows for participation by others in many venues. Presidents have variable influence on policy substance (more on foreign and defense than domestic), policy type (most on crisis response), policy process (most on the early phases of problem definition, agenda designation, and option formulation), and policy coordination (a substantial degree on budgeting, though less than in the past). Finally, the work of presidents has the greatest historical impact as a consequence of unanticipated events that suspend the usual functioning of the separated system. These happenings, typically as crises, come to be the tests of leadership.

Chapter 7
Reform, change, and prospects for the future

The United States and its Constitution are now in their third century. The passage from each century to the next has been eventful. The election of 1800 was bitter and personal. The contest was between two incumbents: John Adams serving as president, Thomas Jefferson as his vice president. Much of the campaign was carried on in the partisan press. Jefferson won with seventy-three electoral votes, but his running mate, Aaron Burr, had an equal number of votes. Burr refused to concede and it took thirty-six ballots in the House of Representatives for Jefferson to win. As a result, power was transferred from the Federalists to the Democratic-Republicans.

The election at the turn into the twentieth century was a rematch between the incumbent Republican president, William McKinley, and the Democratic populist William Jennings Bryan. Many of the difficult issues associated with changes from an agrarian to an industrialized society were being accommodated, if not resolved. New problems were developing that were related to a larger world role for the United States. McKinley, who hardly campaigned, was reelected easily but not overwhelmingly. The two-party system continued to face challenges from third parties, notably the Progressives in the early years of the new century. With McKinley's death by assassination in 1901, a dynamic successor, Theodore ("Teddy") Roosevelt, shouldered the country into the new century.

The 2000 presidential election joined these other "turn of the century" contests as being historic. Democratic Party dominance of Congress had been broken six years earlier, and the election of George W. Bush brought to Washington the first all-Republican government in nearly fifty years. Bush's election was among the most contentious in history, showcasing, as it did, sour relations between an impeached President Clinton and the Republican Congress, and the frustrations of Democrats serving in the minority. Having the election settled by the Supreme Court and Bush losing the popular vote added to an intensely partisan mood in the nation's capital carrying through to the Obama presidency.

These three contests also reveal changes in the presidency. The president's constitutional authority has remained essentially the same, but the circumstances under which this authority is exercised are dramatically different at each century's end. The presidency was being formed when Jefferson was inaugurated. It was more a person than an institution, with the incumbent seeking to comprehend the extent and meaning of his powers.

By 1900 the presidency was beginning its ascendancy. *Congressional Government,* as Woodrow Wilson titled his treatise in 1885, could manage the issues of an agrarian society. Industrialization and growth of the world economy required the professionalism of bureaucracy, hierarchy, and executive control, including that by the chief executive. Take-over President Theodore Roosevelt welcomed these responsibilities, as did Woodrow Wilson and Franklin D. Roosevelt. Other presidents of the first third of the century, Taft, Harding, Coolidge, and Hoover, were less moved to embrace an expansive view of presidential power. Still the die was cast. From FDR forward, the presidency would grow in status, influence, and structure.

In two hundred years, the presidency had changed from that of a person—Washington followed by Adams, then Jefferson—to a presidential enterprise with a cast of thousands. Richard E.

Neustadt expressed it this way as he reviewed *The President at Mid-Century*: "President and presidency are synonymous no longer; the office now comprises an officialdom." The White House remains the symbolic location of the presidency but it can house only a small portion of the presidential workforce. Accordingly, George W. Bush's principal task as president-elect in 2000 was to fill jobs, beginning with a personnel director.

This review suggests an important lesson in considering the presidency in the twenty-first century: Events, the issues they generate, and the people who serve are normally more important than reforms in explaining change. Neustadt again: "The presidency nowadays [has] a different look....But...that look was not conjured up by statutes, or by staffing. These, rather, are *responses* to the impacts of external circumstances upon our form of government; not causes but effects." This lesson should not come as a surprise. After all, the presidency is a vital institution in a representative democracy. As such it may be expected to respond to events, and this includes making adjustments so as to function more effectively.

Reform and change

The presidency is a frequent object of reformers. It is thought by many to be the most powerful branch in the separated system. Therefore, it is excessively credited and blamed, depending on the success or failure of government actions. Of the three branches, Congress is most prone to propose reforms because it competes regularly with the presidency for shares of powers. The judiciary's role in this competition is at a greater distance and depends on the circumstance of a case. Court decisions typically set conditions for reforms, then to be designed by others.

What does reform mean? How does it differ from change? As used here, reforms are major efforts to alter the structure or authority of the presidency. They refer to those cases where the sole intent is to rearrange how the institution works. New authority to implement policy is not included. For example, the Twenty-second Amendment limiting the president to two terms is most definitely a reform; granting the president the authority to set emission standards to improve air quality is not, though it enlarges and thus changes his reach.

Congress, the competing branch, typically proposes root-and-branch institutional reform of the presidency. Members of Congress regularly warn that presidential prerogatives can lead to an "imperial presidency" that distorts the separation of equal powers. Most often such reactions are more rhetorical than aimed at reform.

Reforms seldom produce the desired change. They are typically motivated by disagreement with a substantive decision (for example, to go to war). However, the correction tends to be procedural (for example, to change *how* decisions to commit troops are made). Unfortunately for the reformer, changing organization, rules, or processes is no guarantee of an acceptable outcome. Reforms typically have unanticipated consequences; changes are those consequences.

The distinction between reform and change is found in proposals to improve versus the effects of real-life developments. What is happening in the nation is, and should be, represented in Washington at both ends of Pennsylvania Avenue. Reformers ordinarily have a preferred model of how presidents should behave. But these designs by experts rarely explain the actual responses to events and issues that produce changes in governance.

Selected reforms and their effects

Reforms can be made in several ways: constitutional amendments, statutes, and court decisions. Also varied are the motivations for proposing reforms: correcting a defect, improving a governmental process, reorganizing government, delegating authority, clarifying or limiting authority, reallocating powers, and expanding prerogatives. Reform is sometimes motivated by a judgment that power holders have gone too far in the exercise of their authority and at other times because authority has not been used previously to suit a particular situation. Both urges were illustrated in the aftermath of 9/11 in the effort to manage an unfamiliar war on terrorism. Reformers often aim to make the executive more accountable. Measuring accountability for what happens in a system of divided authority is difficult, yet essential if reform is to be effective. Put differently, separating powers diffuses accountability, thus making it challenging in the extreme to centralize it without rearranging the constitutional order.

Constitutional amendments

Given the complexity of the amending process (requiring supermajorities at both the congressional and state levels), one does not expect it to happen often. There are nine amendments directly affecting the presidency. They are of three types: corrections to omissions or anomalies in the original document, expansions of the voting franchise, and limits on terms of office.

The Twelfth, Twentieth, Twenty-third, and Twenty-fifth Amendments provided needed corrections to the Constitution. The amendments had varying effects. The Twelfth, which stipulated that the Electoral College must vote on the presidential and vice presidential candidates separately, was vital. The Twentieth and Twenty-fifth also had important and desirable effects. Imagine today having the new president take office on March 4, four months after the election, rather than on January 20. A lame-duck president would continue to serve for another six weeks. Remarkably, this change was not made until 1933.

Vice presidents have come to play important roles in recent presidencies, certainly from Carter forward. The provision in the Twenty-fifth amendment for replacing the vice president has been

Table 7.1 Reforms as Constitutional Amendments

Type 1: Correction

Amendment (ratified)	Purpose
Twelfth (1804)	Electors vote separately for president and vice president
Twentieth (1933)	Presidential term ends January 20 rather than March 4 (set by Congress in 1792)
Twenty-third (1961)	District of Columbia provided with three electoral votes
Twenty-fifth (1967)	Fill a vice-presidential vacancy and provide method for managing when the president is unable to discharge duties

Type 2: Expand Voting Franchise

Fifteenth (1870)	Right to vote extended to African Americans
Nineteenth (1920)	Right extended to women
Twenty-fourth (1964)	Right cannot be denied for failure to pay a poll tax
Twenty-sixth (1971)	Age eligibility lowered to 18

Type 3: Two-Term Limitation

Twenty-second (1951)	Presidents limited to two terms

used twice since its inception—installing Gerald Ford when Spiro Agnew resigned in 1973 and Nelson Rockefeller when Ford became president following Nixon's resignation, August 9, 1974. The provision also would have been invoked in 1999 had Clinton been removed by the Senate following his impeachment in the House in 1998. Replacement President Gore would have nominated a vice president to serve with him from 1999 to 2001.

Had Nixon been impeached and removed from office in 1974 (as some Democrats threatened to do prior to Nixon's resignation), there would have been no vice president to take over had the Twenty-fifth Amendment not been passed and ratified. Under those conditions, the Speaker of the House, Carl Albert (D-Oklahoma), would have assumed the presidency, a prospect he did not welcome.

The Fifteenth, Nineteenth, and Twenty-sixth Amendments attuned suffrage to contemporary trends—assuring African Americans and women the right to vote and lowering the eligible age for voting to eighteen. The Twenty-fourth Amendment was a long overdue guarantee of the right to vote without having to pay a poll tax. The suffrage amendments would, over time, transform the nature of presidential campaigns. Each resulted in huge increases in the number of eligible voters.

The one remaining amendment, the Twenty-second, revisited a debate thought to have been settled at the Constitutional Convention. Presidents by custom had limited themselves to two terms. FDR did not. With the end of World War II and the extraordinary executive powers of a president reelected three times, a two-term limitation amendment was introduced soon after the Republican Congress met in 1947. It quickly passed both houses by the required two-thirds majorities and was sent to the states for ratification, which occurred four years later. The effect of the Twenty-second Amendment is uncertain. It first applied to Eisenhower (as the incumbent at the time the amendment was proposed, Truman was excluded from the limitation). Judging its effect requires evaluating an imponderable: Would those presidents serving two full terms seek a third? Age and health likely would have led Eisenhower and Reagan to pass on a third term. That leaves Clinton, George W. Bush, and Obama. In Clinton's case, age might have weighed in favor of his seeking a third term. He was fifty-four at the end of his second term. Having been impeached may well have convinced him otherwise. Bush experienced a sharp drop in his job approval ratings during his second term, which would at the least have provided an incentive for others in his party to challenge his renomination. Obama, too, experienced a notable decline in job approval, though not as seriously as Bush. By reason of age, however, he will leave the White House just a year older than Clinton and might well have seriously considered a third term.

What can be said is that the amendment has replaced a question mark with a period. Will the president seek a third term? He cannot. As a consequence, the election following a reelection will feature open races in both parties. As a consequence, a presidential campaign may be expected to begin soon after the inauguration of the second-term president. Many of the candidates are likely to be serving on Capitol Hill, mostly in the Senate, anxious to augment their records in anticipation of the campaign. Meanwhile, the president's cabinet and staff know their time too is limited, thus encouraging thoughts about their careers. Overcoming this rush to the future so as to manage the present is a major challenge for a term-limited leader, one of those unanticipated consequences of reform—a rush to the exits in the final months.

Statutes

Most reforms and adaptations to change occur through the ordinary lawmaking process. Regular work on Capitol Hill and in the White House is less consciously reformist than simply trying to discover the best or most feasible way to manage the agenda. For example, when programs like the Affordable [Health] Care Act (2010) are put in place over a period of years, Congress authorizes the executive, within limits, to do what is necessary organizationally and procedurally for effective implementation. One consequence of the passage of such massive programs is a significant expansion of the bureaucracy and increased presidential responsibilities. Reform was intended in these cases but directed to health care delivery, not institutional growth. Furthermore, as evident in regard to Obamacare, the amount of executive discretion may be debatable, even subject to decisions by the federal courts (as with the Affordable Care Act: *National Federation of Independent Business v. Sebelius, 2012* and *King v. Burwell, 2015*).

Members of Congress are charged with overseeing the administration of such programs, but in reality they are dependent on the executive, even in the exercise of oversight. That dependency is one measure of the power of the executive in relationship to the legislature.

It is worth noting that presidents do not always welcome these greater responsibilities. In fact, those presidents inheriting entitlement programs may seek to curb their growth because of the effect of uncontrollable spending on the deficit and subsequent debt, which, in turn, limit presidential options for inaugurating new programs.

In addition to legislation on substantive policy matters (for example, agriculture, welfare, health care, and crime), from time to time Congress passes laws that are designed to bolster or constrain presidential prerogatives or affect how presidents do their politics. Such laws are ordinarily more directly reformist in intent than merely the effect of an increase in policy substance to be implemented. Those designing such legislation want to change the "how" and "who" of decision making, not just the "what." There have been many such efforts to reform the presidency and the executive branch in regard to six vital functions: budgeting, the economy, organizational capacity, national security, campaigning, and public access. Most of the laws aim to strengthen or restrict the presidency; some are designed to strengthen Congress so it may compete more effectively with the executive branch.

It is apparent in reviewing these laws that the overall trend is toward a greater role for the president, interspersed by efforts to

Table 7.2 Reforms as Statutes: Selected Cases

Legislation	Reform
Budgeting	
Budget and Accounting Act of 1921	Created first national budget system, established the Bureau of the Budget (BOB)
Congressional Budget and Impoundment, Control Act of 1974	Designed congressional budget, established Congressional Budget Office (CBO), and limited president's authority to impound funds
Gramm-Rudman-Hollings Anti-Deficit Act of 1985	Established automatic spending adjustments with a goal of balancing the budget
Line-item veto of 1996	Authorized a process for the president to veto specific projects. Declared unconstitutional by the Supreme Court
The Economy	
Federal Reserve Act of 1913	Established an independent system for monetary policy, with a Board of Governors
Reciprocal Trade Agreement Act of 1934	Authorized the president to enter into commercial trade agreements with foreign nations
Employment Act of 1946	Created the president's Council of Economic Advisers (CEA) and provided for reports on the state of the economy
Reorganization	
Reorganization Plan of 1939 (and subsequent plans)	Created Executive Office of the President (EOP), moved BOB to EOP (from Treasury), increased presidential staff. Followed by other plans expanding EOP.

(continued)

Table 7.2 Continued

Legislation	Reform
National Security	
National Security Act of 1947	Reorganized the military services into a Department of Defense, created National Security Council (NSC) and staff in EOP, created the Central Intelligence Agency (CIA)
War Powers Act of 1973	Limited president's authority to commit troops to combat. Set timetables for reports and withdrawal when declaration of war lacking. Passed over Nixon's veto
National Commission on Terrorist Attacks, 2002	Authorized appointment of commission to explore intelligence failures prior to 9/11 and to make recommendations
Intelligence Overhaul of 2004	Reorganization of intelligence agencies, authorizing appointment of a director to coordinate intelligence services, including the CIA
Campaigning	
Federal Election Campaign Act of 1974	Provided public funding of presidential campaigns, created Federal Election Commission (FEC)
Bipartisan Campaign Reform Act of 2002	Restrictions on raising soft money and other limits on financing campaigns
Public Access	
Freedom of Information Act Amendments of 1974	Major expansion of the 1966 act providing public access to government documents. Enacted over Ford's veto

check or control such growth. Most of the developments followed logically from the growth and complexity of government programs. Budgeting came to be increasingly important, requiring the expertise of economic and accounting specialists, so that function was concentrated in the executive. Congress became anxious because of its dependency on the executive and formed its own process in 1974, which included hiring its own budget specialists.

Similar trends are noted in regard to the economy, national security policy, and the institutionalization of the presidency. Presidents are commonly held responsible for the state of the economy, even though they have limited tools for managing it. Thus, for example, the independent Federal Reserve Board has substantially more authority than cabinet departments or agencies to influence economic developments by its role in monetary policy. Congress has authorized support for economic management, and presidents have reorganized within the White House for this purpose (the formation of a National Economic Council in 1993 by executive order being one such change).

The responsibility of the president for national security policy has a constitutional basis within his role as commander in chief. Organizational unity of the military services in the Department of Defense was supplemented by the creation of a National Security Council and staff in 1947. As with budgeting, Congress has from time to time expressed concern about the president's dominance in this area and has thus increased its efforts to limit military engagements without a declaration of war and to investigate national security decision making when things go wrong. These actions are not without effect, but the president continues to lead when it comes to foreign and national security policy.

The presidency has undoubtedly grown as an institution. The critical point came in 1939 with the creation of the Executive Office of the President (EOP). The name itself acknowledged the need for an umbrella organization to shelter the many advisory units required to match the growth of government programs. And so with each extension—national security, the economy, the environment, trade, science—another "office" or "council" joined the all-important Office of Management and Budget in the EOP. Taken together with the White House Office, these are the units that form the presidential branch.

Two other types of statutes concern campaigning and public access. The first is most often a story of frustration for reformers. They pay attention primarily to campaign finance, the concern being the amount of money spent and its sources. New laws change how money is raised, but they have not curbed the amounts and have had variable effects on who gives. As to access, the Freedom of Information Act, as amended, has benefited the media and scholars while encouraging caution within the executive branch about producing and preserving documents.

These statutes illustrate the intricate politics of reform in a separated powers government. Ever attentive to institutional status, the branches protect their prerogatives and often resent those of others. Accordingly, designs for change in response to events and agenda shifts are scrutinized carefully at both ends of Pennsylvania Avenue for how they affect the balance of powers.

What are the effects and lessons of statutory reform? It is apparent that representative government will respond to what goes on outside the capital. It is logical, for example, for executives to prepare budgets and manage the military. And that is what has occurred, even though it reduces the influence of the representative legislature. Logic has dictated the expansion of the executive during the twentieth and into the twenty-first centuries. Many statutes have resulted in greater responsibilities for presidents (if not necessarily greater powers)—regarding the budget, the military, war making, the economy, and social issues. Just as evident is the failure of Congress to keep pace. Members have tried by creating their own budget process, reorganizing committees, expanding staff, adding legislative agencies, and demanding more executive accountability. But the challenges are immense in preparing legislation and overseeing its implementation. It is well-nigh impossible to turn back the clock. The War Powers Act (1973) illustrates that fact well. War has been in the process of redefinition for decades. The most recent iteration—the war on terrorism—has stimulated further debate and puzzlement regarding the sharing of powers between the branches.

Supreme Court decisions

The third source of reform and change to the presidency is the Supreme Court. Justices in that body are not reformers by the nature of their jobs. Whatever their personal beliefs, their judicial status and place of work do not foster their taking reform initiatives. Yet their decisions can have the effect of enhancing, clarifying, or thwarting authority exercised by the president. It is generally accepted that the Supreme Court will uphold executive powers. After all, not to do so is a case of one branch overruling another. Those occasions, when they happen, do engage the attention of the public.

At least three types of decisions can have an effect on presidential power. First are decisions that strike down law favored by the president but judged by the Supreme Court to exceed his authority. For example, President Franklin D. Roosevelt proposed bold legislation to deal with the Great Depression. Several programs were struck down by the Supreme Court, notably a proposal in the National Industrial Recovery Act to set industry codes of fair competition (*Schechter Poultry Corporation v. United States*, 1935) and provisions of the Agriculture Adjustment Act (*United States v. Butler*, 1936).

Second are decisions regarding legislation proposed by others. The Federal Election Campaign Act Amendments of 1974 were proposed and passed during the Watergate scandals. Among their many provisions, the amendments set contribution and spending limits. The Supreme Court declared the latter in violation of the First Amendment right of free speech (*Buckley v. Valeo*, 1976). The ruling meant that campaign expenditures would continue to escalate, making it imperative that presidential candidates have access to huge sums of money. Decades later the Court in *Citizens United v.*

Federal Election Commission (2010) likewise found restrictions in the Bipartisan Campaign Reform Act of 2002 to violate the First Amendment. Further increases in campaign funding followed.

Third are those decisions the Supreme Court wishes to avoid but may well require their attention: those involving uses of executive authority. It is difficult to generalize about these decisions for predicting future outcomes, apart from the Supreme Court's attention to presidential overreaching in dealing with unprecedented situations.

Removals of presidential appointees were the subjects of the *Myers* and *Humphries* cases. Clarification was essential as new agencies and appointment procedures were instituted. The *Myers* decision allowed removal of those appointed by the president with Senate concurrence; the *Humphries* decision restricted removal of those in a growing number of independent regulatory commissions.

Two cases involved unprecedented wartime situations. During the Korean War, President Truman was concerned that a pending strike against the steel industry would harm the production of needed war materiel. Truman ordered the seizure of the mills, presumably relying on his powers as commander in chief. The Court rejected Truman's interpretation of his authority. Much later, President George W. Bush faced the exceptional circumstance of trying alleged or suspected terrorists with no common national identity. His solution was to establish separate military tribunals, done without requesting congressional approval. Again the Court rejected Bush's interpretation of presidential authority while inviting Congress to act (*Hamdan v. Rumsfeld*), as it did late in the 109th Congress by providing for military commissions to prosecute terrorism suspects.

United States v. Nixon and *Clinton v. Jones* were special as cases in which the president sought to prevent potentially damaging evidence from entering the judicial process. Nixon invoked executive privilege to prevent tapes of Oval Office conversations from being used by the Watergate special prosecutor. The Court

Table 7.3 Interpreting Presidential Power: Selected Supreme Court Cases

Case	Decision
Myers v. United States (1926)	President does not need Senate approval to remove those appointed with Senate approval
Humphries Executor v. United States (1935)	Limited the president's power to remove members of independent regulatory commissions
Youngstown Sheet & Tube Co. v. Sawyer (1952)	Declared President Truman's seizure of steel mills during the Korean War an unconstitutional act
United States v. Nixon (1974)	Rejected President Nixon's claim of executive privilege in refusing to turn over Oval Office tapes to the special prosecutor
Clinton v. Jones (1997)	Incumbent president is not protected by the Constitution from civil litigation; suit by Paula Jones can go forward
Clinton et al. v. New York City et al. (1998)	Line-item veto provided to president by Congress is unconstitutional
Bush v. Gore (2000)	Recount procedures designated by the Florida Supreme Court were unconstitutional (holding applied to the present case)
Hamdan v. Rumsfeld (2006)	Military commissions established by President Bush to try suspected terrorists are unconstitutional

rejected his claim, which eventually led to Nixon's resignation. Clinton wished to prevent a civil action by Paula Jones, a former Arkansas state employee, from going forward while he was still in office. The Court decided such an action would not interfere with the exercise of presidential duties. Both cases were unanimously decided against the president.

The other two cases display the diversity of what comes before the Supreme Court. The Republican Congress provided for a line-item veto during Clinton's presidency, authority he asked for, as had presidents of both parties before him. In *Clinton et al. v. New York City et al.* the Court could find no constitutional basis for such authority. And in 2000 the Court decided to halt the Florida recount and, for all practical purposes, award the presidency to George W. Bush. Sensitive to the extraordinary circumstance of resolving a presidential election dispute, the Court emphasized that its decision applied only to the present case, the 2000 election.

Court decisions regarding the presidency are not reforms as much as clarifications with implications for change. When Congress and the president make adaptations to suit new or developing circumstances, the Court may accept a case asking it to judge whether such actions meet constitutional muster. *Marbury v. Madison* (1803) is cited in some of these cases: "It is emphatically the province and duty of the judicial department to say what the law is." Thus, for example, if a president claims to have executive privilege or asserts that a decision is in accordance with inherent powers, the Court may hear a challenge and decide whether the president is correct.

Perhaps the broadest lesson for presidents from this review is this: When in doubt, rely on the separation of powers. Primarily that message suggests getting congressional approval or judicial clearance (at minimum by carefully examining court precedents). It advises against going it alone except in crises where time is of the essence. A related lesson is that presidents should be cautious about asserting powers to protect themselves against charges regarding their personal behavior. When this happens, presidents, rather than the courts, are saying what the law is.

Customs and expectations

Changes in customs and what the public and others expect of the presidency also have powerful effects. These features are more amorphous than constitutional amendments, statutes, or Court

10. President Franklin D. Roosevelt's joint wartime press conference with British prime minister Winston Churchill on December 23, 1941.

decisions, yet no less indicative of governmental, political, and societal developments. Customs are ordinary ways of doing things, as with habits or routines. New circumstances typically establish new customs. For example, FDR met twice a week with reporters in the Oval Office. They crowded around his desk to ask questions. His responses were ordinarily off the record. Apart from major addresses, Roosevelt's communication with the public was also low key. He inaugurated fireside chats on the radio, a new and popular form of presidential communication with the public, also convenient for him given his disability.

The transformation in communications and travel dramatically changed how presidents and their staffs now interact with the press and public. Meetings with reporters are not only on the record for the press but are typically viewed as well by anyone who has an interest. Video and transcripts are available on websites.

Presidents travel with greater frequency than ever, campaigning for public support of their programs. President Clinton went on the road immediately after delivering his State of the Union messages to justify and defend his proposals, a practice that has come to be "customary" for his successors, George W. Bush and Barack Obama, and is likely to continue.

The customary roles of those in the White House entourage have changed markedly. In the past, First Ladies were seldom judged to be public figures in their own right (Eleanor Roosevelt being a major exception). Not anymore. Vice presidents had few functions, little staff, and no official residence. State of the Union messages were sent to Congress in writing, not delivered there by the president. And decades back, security at the White House was lax; citizens could walk in freely. All of that, and more, has changed.

These developments have also contributed to altered expectations of the president and the presidency. Expectations may be in two forms: those associated with what the press and public come to know about the person's background, philosophy, and values; the anticipations related to the presidency—notably its leadership role in the separated system and its status in the world. These two images are not always in harmony and can change during a president's time in office.

Truman, for example, had to deal with incongruous expectations— low for him due to his lack of executive experience; high for the presidency following the three-plus terms of FDR. Eisenhower's background as a military leader was expected to restore the positive image of the presidency following scandals in the Truman administration. Watergate and its aftermath (including President Ford's pardon of Nixon) had a negative effect on the image of the presidency, thus creating a major challenge for Carter, a president with no Washington experience. The first Bush was among the most qualified presidents by the measure of executive experience, but his presidency was shaped by expectations born of the forceful leadership style of his predecessor, Ronald Reagan. The second Bush was confronted with a presidency diminished by Clinton's impeachment, yet one facing questions about Bush's competence to lead and the legitimacy of his victory. It was expected that Obama's presidency would be "post-partisan," working cooperatively across the aisle but quite the opposite occurred as partisanship dominated presidential-congressional relations.

Looking ahead: the new realities

The future of the presidency is heavily influenced by its past and present. The most reliable way to look ahead is through the prism of current politics. The constitutional state of the presidency has undergone relatively few changes. The most important of these alterations—the two-term limitation—occurred in the mid-twentieth century. Apart from the quadrennial proposals to reform the Electoral College, no serious amendments to Article II are contemplated. And so the core function—"The executive power shall be vested in a President of the United States of America"—remains the same.

What has changed is the context within which executive power is exercised. That is true through history. What in the present setting aids in predicting the future? The political, policy, and administrative landscapes are notably relevant in assessing presidential power in this new century.

Political

Little or nothing in the political landscape suggests change in the narrow margins that have been featured in presidential and congressional election results since 1992. The shift from a strongly Democratic South to Republican dominance in that region has solidified an intensely competitive national two-party system. The tight split is indicated by a red state/blue state map and referred to with a shorthand phrase: *polarization*. Much of the analysis has a reformist tinge in suggesting that the split is a condition to be corrected. In reality, presidential and congressional elections are likely to be closely decided and not very subject to manipulation on a national scale.

Narrow margins can easily result in split-party government. One senator leaving his party for independent status in 2001 shifted Senate majority control from the Republicans to the Democrats. With changes in a few votes in Florida in 2000 and Ohio in 2004, the Democrats would have won the White House, very likely both times with a Republican Congress. The 2006 midterm elections resulted in a 49–49 tie in the Senate, with two independents voting with the Democrats to organize the chamber.

These realities have had a profound effect on the presidency. The incentives in the White House and Congress are competitive and partisan, not cooperative and bipartisan. Presidents have to design strategies accounting for small margins, partisanship, and intense competition, yet be prepared to compromise at key junctures in the lawmaking process and to act forcefully in responding to crises. Presidents in narrow-margin politics are likely also to be attentive to the importance of party discipline in Congress, taking care not to undermine House and Senate leadership efforts by entering into cross-party agreements in the early stages of lawmaking. The "dance of legislation," as one analyst called it, is fanciful.

The partisan incentives of narrow margins and split control are likely to be pervasive, with a potent congressional minority exercising every available tactic to force compromise or obstruct. The more active the minority, the more the majority seeks additional partisan advantages, often now in both chambers. These conditions frequently result in a reduced role for the president, who, rather than merely serving as an observer, may seek to govern executively by orders or rule making. Regularizing such methods may deform the separated powers system, bypassing Congress.

However unappealing, this landscape need not be perilous to lawmaking. Laws do get enacted, crises overcome partisanship, and both parties, not just the governing party, have incentives to participate actively in policymaking. The point is that the context for exercising presidential power is different. It is also perfectly legitimate in a system of separated powers.

Policy

Subject as it is to events, the policy agenda is ever changing. Predictions are therefore somewhat less supportable than with a more stable political landscape. For example, what had settled into a primarily domestic set of issues during the Clinton presidency and into the early months of George W. Bush's first term was dramatically altered by 9/11. That event spawned issues that appear to "have legs." Accordingly, it is likely that future presidents will face the policy uncertainties of unfamiliar war making.

Perhaps foremost of these sureties is the effect of national security on the rest of the agenda. Terrorism has had an acute effect as a dominant issue in and of itself, and for its influence on how other issues are defined. For itself, combating terrorism involves a stateless war, one in which the enemy may be concealed within several countries, including the United States. More broadly, it profoundly affects issues such as immigration, port security, international trade and finance, and federal-state-local policing functions, to name a few.

An issue of such wide-ranging proportions will elicit serious debate and criticism. The adage from earlier times that such debate should stop at the water's edge, preferably with bipartisan support for the president, no longer holds. Almost by definition, rules based on what is known (for example, conventional war) are difficult to apply to the unfamiliar (for example, a stateless war on terrorism). Future presidents cannot expect national security and foreign policy decisions to receive automatic approval by Congress, the media, or the public, possibly apart from a catastrophe akin to that of 9/11.

The war on terrorism, American military and political engagements in the Middle East, and the development of nuclear weapons capabilities in unfriendly regimes have influenced how domestic issues are interpreted by policymakers. Yet there are other realities associated with homeland issues. Most such matters derive from programs already on the books. "Reform" is incorporated into nearly all major presidential proposals: Social Security reform, Medicare reform, immigration reform, environmental reform. The domestic agenda is primarily generated from what the government is already doing. That fact is unlikely to change with a new administration.

Article II of the US Constitution is brief. There is no lengthy list of presidential powers, as is found for Congress in Article I. Presidents depend more on persuasion and executive programmatic growth than detailed constitutional authority. They are held responsible for achieving unity in the separated system, having won the position and location to accomplish that goal. Such is the future, as it has been the past.

Administrative

The costs of entitlements and military preparedness have increased exponentially with limited or no controls. Spending has become automatic. Formulas and events determine expenditures, with revenues failing to keep pace and narrow-margin politics making it difficult either to raise taxes or reduce benefits. Deficits result and the public debt increases. President Clinton and a Republican Congress made an effort in 1997 to demonstrate how future budgets might be balanced, but events and politics prevailed to set record deficits and debt after 2001.

A famous western song is titled "Don't Fence Me In." It is no exaggeration to imagine presidential power as "fenced in." Presidents are managers of debt. They make promises during campaigns but can keep them only when they find revenue-neutral means for implementing them, convince Congress that the programs promised justify adding to the national debt, or cutting expenditures elsewhere in order to do something new.

Less noticed as an administrative development is the federalization of government programs. Presidents and their appointees administer much of the domestic agenda through two, three, or more layers of government. Thus, for example, the national health care program, dubbed "Obamacare," is administered through a complex network of exchanges, some created by the states, others for states by the national Department of Health and Human Services. The Department of Homeland Security cooperates with and directs state and local law enforcement organizations. Small wonder the White House has developed its own branch of specialists. Presidents want and need assistants who will guide them through the pathways of program development, enactment, and delivery. The White House has long since ceased to be merely the Executive Mansion. It is now the branch of government struggling to manage that for which presidents will be held accountable.

Learning to be president

It is said that all presidents learn on the job, starting with their first briefing on pending issues. Put otherwise, no one enters the White House fully prepared to go to work. Orientations are essential. Furthermore, newly elected presidents have just experienced two extraordinarily ego-centric occurrences—a successful election campaign, followed by celebration and inauguration. There is, at that point, much to learn about being president, and much to set aside from the campaign to get there.

Next to ponder is what exactly has been won. It is, foremost, a position and location from which to persuade others. Thus, for example, regardless of the size of the win, the planks of the platform were not themselves voted on. Rather, the new president was given more or less political capital to use with others in winning their endorsement.

Related is consideration of who else won. The separated system is rooted in a division of legitimacy based on different election schedules and term lengths among the winners. Accordingly, the president's party may win the White House only, or half of the congressional branch, or both branches but then lose all or part at the midterm two years later. Policy strategies must account for these variations in how voters make their choices in legitimizing the elected branches of the separated system.

Above all, the president was charged with achieving unity within the separated system, accepting the conditions set by the Founders. Doing so has always been challenging but often intensely so in the post–World War II era of frequent split-party government and narrow margins. It would be beneficial in this regard to recall this adage: *The president is not the presidency; the presidency is not the government; ours is not a presidential, but rather a separated, system.*

Professor E. Pendleton Herring described the presidency so well: "We have created a position of great power but have made the full realization of that power dependent upon *influence* rather than legal authority." Accordingly, study of the institution must acknowledge the president's political status and style within the constitutional structure.

Appendix
Presidents and Vice Presidents of the United States of America

Year	President	Vice President	Party	Vote %
1789	George Washington	John Adams	Federalist	EV = 100*
1792	George Washington	John Adams	Federalist	EV = 98
1796	John Adams	Thomas Jefferson	Federalist/ Democratic Republican**	EV = 51
1800	Thomas Jefferson	Aaron Burr	Democratic Republican	EV = 53***
1804	Thomas Jefferson	George Clinton	Democratic Republican	EV = 92
1808	James Madison	George Clinton	Democratic Republican	EV = 69
1812	James Madison	Elbridge Gerry	Democratic Republican	EV = 59
1816	James Monroe	Daniel D. Tompkins	Democratic Republican	EV = 83
1820	James Monroe	Daniel D. Tompkins	Democratic Republican	EV = 98

(continued)

Presidents and Vice Presidents of the United States of America

Year	President	Vice President	Party	Vote %
1824	John Quincy Adams	John C. Calhoun	Democratic Republican	PV = 31 EV = 32***
1828	Andrew Jackson	John C. Calhoun	Democratic Republican	PV = 56 EV = 68
1832	Andrew Jackson	Martin Van Buren	Democrat	PV = 54 EV = 76
1836	Martin Van Buren	Richard M. Johnson	Democrat	PV = 51 EV = 58
1840	William Henry Harrison	John Tyler*	Whig	PV = 53 EV = 80
1844	James K. Polk	George M. Dallas	Democrat	PV = 50 EV = 62
1848	Zachary Taylor	Millard Fillmore*	Whig	PV = 47 EV = 56
1852	Franklin Pierce	William R. King	Democrat	PV = 51 EV = 86
1856	James Buchanan	John C. Breckinridge	Democrat	PV = 45 EV = 59
1860	Abraham Lincoln	Hannibal Hamlin	Republican	PV = 40 EV = 59
1864	Abraham Lincoln	Andrew Johnson*	Republican	PV = 55 EV = 91
1868	Ulysses S. Grant	Schuyler Colfax	Republican	PV = 53 EV = 73
1872	Ulysses S. Grant	Henry Wilson	Republican	PV = 56 EV = 78

Year	President	Vice President	Party	Vote %
1876	Rutherford B. Hayes	William A. Wheeler	Republican	PV = 48 EV = 50+
1880	James A. Garfield	Chester A. Arthur*	Republican	PV = 48 EV = 58
1884	Grover Cleveland	Thomas A. Hendricks	Democrat	PV = 49 EV = 55
1888	Benjamin Harrison	Levi P. Morton	Republican	PV = 48 EV = 58
1892	Grover Cleveland	Adlai E. Stevenson	Democrat	PV = 46 EV = 62
1896	William McKinley	Garret Hobart	Republican	PV = 51 EV = 61
1900	William McKinley	Theodore Roosevelt*	Republican	PV = 52 EV = 65
1904	Theodore Roosevelt	Charles W. Fairbanks	Republican	PV = 56 EV = 71
1908	William Howard Taft	James S. Sherman	Republican	PV = 52 EV = 66
1912	Woodrow Wilson	Thomas Marshall	Democrat	PV = 42 EV = 82
1916	Woodrow Wilson	Thomas Marshall	Democrat	PV = 49 EV = 52
1920	Warren Harding	Calvin Coolidge*	Republican	PV = 60 EV = 76
1924	Calvin Coolidge	Charles G. Dawes	Republican	PV = 54 EV = 72

(continued)

Presidents and Vice Presidents of the United States of America

Year	President	Vice President	Party	Vote %
1928	Herbert C. Hoover	Charles Curtis	Republican	PV = 58 EV = 84
1932	Franklin D. Roosevelt	John Nance Garner	Democrat	PV = 57 EV = 89
1936	Franklin D. Roosevelt	John Nance Garner	Democrat	PV = 61 EV = 98
1940	Franklin D. Roosevelt	Henry A. Wallace	Democrat	PV = 55 EV = 85
1944	Franklin D. Roosevelt	Harry S. Truman*	Democrat	PV = 53 EV = 81
1948	Harry S. Truman	Alben W. Barkley	Democrat	PV = 50 EV = 57
1952	Dwight D. Eisenhower	Richard Nixon	Republican	PV = 55 EV = 83
1956	Dwight D. Eisenhower	Richard Nixon	Republican	PV = 57 EV = 86
1960	John F. Kennedy	Lyndon B. Johnson*	Democrat	PV = 50 EV = 56
1964	Lyndon B. Johnson	Hubert Humphrey	Democrat	PV = 61 EV = 90
1968	Richard Nixon	Spiro Agnew	Republican	PV = 43 EV = 56
1972	Richard Nixon	Spiro Agnew/Gerald Ford**	Republican	PV = 61 EV = 97
1976	Jimmy Carter	Walter Mondale	Democrat	PV = 50 EV = 55

Year	President	Vice President	Party	Vote %
1980	Ronald Reagan	George H. W. Bush	Republican	PV = 51 EV = 91
1984	Ronald Reagan	George H. W. Bush	Republican	PV = 59 EV = 98
1988	George H. W. Bush	James Danforth Quayle	Republican	PV = 53 EV = 79
1992	William Jefferson (Bill) Clinton	Albert Gore Jr.	Democrat	PV = 43 EV = 69
1996	William Jefferson (Bill) Clinton	Albert Gore Jr.	Democrat	PV = 49 EV = 70
2000	George W. Bush	Richard Cheney	Republican	PV = 48 EV = 50+
2004	George W. Bush	Richard Cheney	Republican	PV = 51 EV = 53
2008	Barack Obama	Joseph Biden	Democrat	PV = 53 EV = 68
2012	Barack Obama	Joseph Biden	Democrat	PV = 51 EV = 62

KEY:

PV = Popular vote percentage

EV = Electoral vote percentage

* Popular vote tabulations were not provided until 1824; electoral vote percentage is for the president only; those running second were vice presidents and received a different percentage until the ratification of the Twelfth Amendment.

** Jefferson, running second and serving as vice president, had a different party affiliation.

*** Election went to the House of Representatives.

This sign indicates a takeover president due to the death of the president.

Agnew resigned as vice president; Ford was appointed under the procedures of the Twenty-second Amendment, then became president when Nixon resigned.

References

Chapter 1

Raoul Berger, *Impeachment: The Constitutional Problems* (Cambridge, MA: Harvard University Press, 1973), 54.

Chapter 2

Stephen Skowronek, *The Politics Presidents Make: Leadership from John Adams to George Bush* (Cambridge, MA: Harvard University Press, 1993), 18.

Chapter 4

Charles O. Jones, *Passages to the Presidency: From Campaigning to Governing* (Washington, DC: Brookings Institution Press, 1998), 52.

Lyndon B. Johnson, *Vantage Point: Perspectives on the Presidency, 1963–1969* (New York: Holt, Rinehart and Winston, 1971), 450.

Chapter 5

Gary Wills quoted in Charles O. Jones, "The Presidency and the Press," *Journal of the Press and Politics* 1, no. 2 (1996), 16.

Charles O. Jones, ed., *Preparing to Be President: The Memos of Richard E. Neustadt* (Washington, DC: American Enterprise Institute Press, 2000), 131.

Lady Bird Johnson quoted in the website of the National First Ladies'
    Library (http://www.firstladies.org/).
George E. Reedy, *The Twilight of the Presidency* (New York: World
    Publishing, 1970), xiv.

Chapter 6

Bob Woodward, *Bush at War* (New York: Simon & Schuster,
    2002), 136.
Ralph K. Huitt, "Democratic Leadership in the Senate," *American
    Political Science Review* 55 (June 1961), 337.
House Republican quoted in Stephen J. Wayne, *The Legislative
    Presidency* (New York: Harper and Row, 1978), 161.

Chapter 7

E. Pendleton Herring, *Presidential Leadership* (New York: Rinehart,
    1940), 2–3.

Further reading

Aberbach, Joel D., and Mark Peterson, eds. *The Executive Branch.* New York: Oxford University Press, 2005.

Arnold, Peri E. *Making the Managerial Presidency: Comprehensive Reorganization Planning, 1905–1996.* 2nd ed. Lawrence: University Press of Kansas, 1998.

Barber, James David. *The Presidential Character: Predicting Performance in the White House.* Englewood Cliffs, NJ: Prentice-Hall, 1992.

Berger, Raoul. *Impeachment: The Constitutional Problems.* Cambridge, MA: Harvard University Press, 1973.

Birnbaum, Jeffrey H. *Madhouse: The Private Turmoil of Working for the President.* New York: Times Books, 1996.

Burke, John P. *The Institutional Presidency.* Baltimore, MD: Johns Hopkins University Press, 1992.

Casper, Gerhard. *Separating Power: Essays on the Founding Period.* Cambridge, MA: Harvard University Press, 1997.

Ceaser, James W. *Presidential Selection: Theory and Development.* Princeton, NJ: Princeton University Press, 1979.

Cook, Rhodes. *The Presidential Nominating Process: A Place for Us?* Lanham, MD: Rowman and Littlefield, 2004.

DeGregorio, William A. *The Complete Book of U.S. Presidents.* New York: Gramercy Books, 2005.

Edwards, George C. III. *Overreach: Leadership in the Obama Presidency.* Princeton, NJ: Princeton University Press, 2012.

Edwards, George C. III, and Stephen J. Wayne. *Presidential Leadership: Politics and Policy Making.* Belmont, CA: Wadsworth, 2013.

Ellis, Richard J., ed. *Founding the American Presidency*. Landam, MD: Rowman and Littlefield, 1999.

Greenstein, Fred I. *Inventing the Job of President: Leadership Style from George Washington to Andrew Jackson*. Princeton, NJ: Princeton University Press, 2009.

Greenstein, Fred I., ed. *Leadership in the Modern Presidency*. Cambridge, MA: Harvard University Press, 1988.

Hamilton, Alexander, John Jay, and James Madison. *The Federalist*. New York: Modern Library, 1937.

Hargrove, Erwin C. *The Effective Presidency: Lessons on Leadership from John F. Kennedy to George W. Bush*. Boulder, CO: Paradigm, 2008.

Hargrove, Erwin C., and Michael Nelson. *Presidents, Politics, and Policy*. Baltimore, MD: Johns Hopkins University Press, 1984.

Hart, John. *The Presidential Branch: From Washington to Clinton*. 2nd ed. New York: Seven Bridges Press/Chatham House, 1995.

Herring, Pendleton. *Presidential Leadership: The Political Relations of Congress and the Chief Executive*. 2nd ed. New Brunswick, NJ: Transaction, 2006.

Hess, Stephen, and James P. Pfiffner. *Organizing the Presidency*. Washington, DC: Brookings Institution Press, 2002.

Jones, Charles O. *Passages to the Presidency: From Campaigning to Governing*. Washington, DC: Brookings Institution Press, 1998.

Jones, Charles O. *The Presidency in a Separated System*. 2nd ed. Washington, DC: Brookings Institution Press, 2005.

Kelly, Alfred H., and Winfred A. Harbison. *The American Constitution: Its Origin and Development*. New York: W. W. Norton, 1948.

Kessel, John H. *Presidents, the Presidency, and the Political Environment*. Washington, DC: CQ Press, 2001.

Kettl, Donald F. *Deficit Politics: Public Budgeting and Its Constitutional and Historical Context*. New York: Macmillan, 1992.

Kumar, Martha Joynt, and Terry Sullivan, eds. *The White House World: Transition, Organization and Office Operations*. College Station: Texas A&M University Press, 2003.

Leuchtenburg, William. *The American President: From Teddy Roosevelt to Bill Clinton*. New York: Oxford University Press, 2015.

Light, Paul C. *The President's Agenda: Domestic Policy Choice from Kennedy to Reagan*. Baltimore, MD: Johns Hopkins University Press, 1991.

Maraniss, David. *Barack Obama: The Story.* New York: Simon & Schuster, 2012.

McDonald, Forrest. *The American Presidency: An Intellectual History.* Lawrence: University Press of Kansas, 1994.

Milkus, Sidney, and Michael Nelson. *The American Presidency: Origins and Development, 1776–2014.* Washington, DC: Congressional Quarterly Press, 2015.

Mutch, Robert. *Buying the Vote.* New York: Oxford University Press, 2015.

Nelson, Michael, ed. *Guide to the Presidency.* 2nd ed. Washington, DC: Congressional Quarterly Press, 1996.

Neustadt, Richard E. *Presidential Power: The Politics of Leadership.* New York: John Wiley, 1960.

Patterson, Bradley H. Jr. *Ring of Power: Inside the West Wing and Beyond.* Washington, DC: Brookings Institution Press, 2000.

Pfiffner, James P. *The Strategic Presidency: Hitting the Ground Running.* 2nd ed. Lawrence: University Press of Kansas, 1996.

Pious, Richard. *Why Presidents Fail: White House Decision Making from Eisenhower to Bush II.* New York: Rowman and Littlefield, 2013.

Powell, William G. *Thinking about the Presidency: The Primacy of Power.* Princeton, NJ: Princeton University Press, 2015.

Robinson, Donald R. *"To the Best of My Ability": The Presidency and the Constitution.* New York: W. W. Norton, 1987.

Schlesinger, Arthur M. Jr. *The Imperial Presidency.* New York: Houghton Mifflin, 1973.

Shull, Steven A. *Domestic Policy Formation: Presidential-Congressional Partnership?* Westport, CT: Greenwood, 1983.

Siemers, David J. *Ratifying the Republic: Antifederalists and Federalists in Constitutional Time.* Stanford, CA: Stanford University Press, 2002.

Skowronek, Stephen. *The Politics Presidents Make: Leadership from John Adams to George Bush.* Cambridge, MA: Harvard University Press, 1993.

White, Leonard D. *The Federalists: A Study of Administrative History.* New York: Macmillan, 1948.

Wildavsky, Aaron. *The New Politics of the Budgetary Process.* Medina, OH: Scott, Foresman, 1988.

Further reading

Index

A

Adams, John, 26, 36, 43–44,
46, 47
Adams, John Quincy, 47–48
Adams, Sherman, 81
Affordable Care Act, 92, 165.
See also health care. Obama
and, 68, 83, 114, 122–23,
149–50
Agnew, Spiro, 147
Agriculture Adjustment Act, 155
Albert, Carl, 148
Albright, Madeleine, 70
American Association of Retired
Persons (AARP), 127
Americorps, 118–19, 127
Anti-Federalists, 4, 7, 10, 13, 28
Anti-Masonic Party, 48
appointments, 27, 28–30, 31, 32,
90, 93; Article II and, 68–69;
cabinet and, 67–70, 78;
Constitution of the United States
on, 43; presidents-elect and,
73–77; of Supreme Court
members, 15, 21, 35, 77; power to
make, 14–16, 21, 36; second-term,
81–82, 83
Arthur, Chester, 56, 59, 60
Article, I 13–14, 21, 112, 135, 164

Article II, 21, 26, 33, 45, 68–69, 77,
85, 161, 164
Article III, 5, 13–14, 77, 136
Articles of Confederation, 2, 4, 8–9,
17, 20, 28
Aspin, Les, 89
Axelrod, David, 99–100

B

Biden, Joseph, 100–101
Bipartisan Campaign Reform Act
(2002), 152, 156
Birnbaum, Jeffrey H., 107
Brady gun control law, 118–19
branches of government, 31, 90, 110;
balance of, 16, 26–28; in capital,
24–26; Congress and, 6, 23;
Founding Fathers and, 20–22;
treaties and, 18; war declarations
and, 16–17. *See also* separation of
powers.
Bryan, William Jennings, 142
Buchanan, James, 56, 61
Buckley v. Valeo, 155
budget, 88, 89
Budget and Accounting Act (1921),
137, 151
Bureau of the Budget (BOB), 94,
95, 137, 151

Bureau of the Census, 92
Burr, Aaron, 43, 45, 46, 142
Bush, Barbara, 102
Bush, George, H. W., 69, 100;
    election and, 40, 60, 64;
    split-party government and, 56;
    transition of, 74, 75
Bush, George, W., 27, 40, 56, 60, 70,
    77; campaign of, 72, 73, 115;
    Congress and, 113; on decision
    making, 111; elections and, 47, 61,
    64; enactments of, 116; historic
    presidency of, 117, 119–22,
    124–25; in polls, 58, 59
Bush, Laura, 102–3
Bush v. Gore, 119, 157
Butler, Pierce, 3–4
Byrnes, John, 133

C

Cabinet, 32, 71, 89, 106, 115, 149;
    appointments and, 67–70, 78;
    president-elect and, 74–75;
    separation of powers and, 78;
    turnover in, 77–80; campaigning,
    71, 114, 118, 150, 152, 155;
    Bush, G. W. and, 72, 73, *115*
Camp David, 125
Cannon, Lou, 113
Carter, Jimmy, 38, 39, 70, 74–75,
    100; Congress and, 113; elections
    and, 60, 61, 73; expectations for,
    40; vice presidency and, 64
Carter, Rosalynn, 102
Central Intelligence Agency (CIA),
    152
checks and balances, 2, 3, 13, 22,
    31, 32
Cheney, Richard, 77, 100, 101, 102
chief of state, 104–6
Churchill, Winston, *159*
*Citizens United v. Federal Election
    Commission*, 155–56
Civil War, 36

Clay, Henry, 47
Cleveland, Grover, 35, 56, 60, 61
Clinton, Bill, 60, 73, 74–75, 100,
    113, 114; election of, 35, 55, 56,
    61; enactments of, 116; health
    care and, 39, 111, 119, 133;
    historic presidency of, 117–19,
    124–25; impeachment and, 11,
    13, 82, 119, 161; scandal and, 38,
    82; transition of, 74–75
Clinton, George, 10, 46
Clinton, Hillary, 102, 103–4
*Clinton et al. v. New York City
    et al.*, 157
Clinton v. Jones, 157
Cohen, William, 69
Cold War, 140
commander in chief, 16, 21, 31,
    32, 109
Committee of Detail, 6–7, 16, 28,
    29, 30; impeachment and, 13; on
    legislative role of president,
    19–20; on veto power, 18–19
Committee of States, 2, 8
Committee of Style, 19
Committee of the Whole, 6
Committee on Administrative
    Management, 98
Committee on Postponed Matters, 7,
    11, 13, 17, 29
Communications, 49–51, 73, 92,
    98, 99, 105, 137, 159–60.
    See also media.
Congress, 29, 30, 31–34, 37, 113;
    appointments and, 14–16;
    branches of government and, 6,
    23; budget and, 23, 112, 138;
    elections and, 21, 54, 65;
    enactments of, 116; in executive
    selection, 14; polls and, 58, 59;
    Electoral College and, 7–8, 21,
    44–45; enactments of, 116;
    separation of powers and, 4, 6,
    21, 28, 109; split-party
    government and, 55, 63

Congressional Budget and Impoundment Control Act (1974), 38, 137–38, 151
Congressional Budget Office (CBO), 96, 137–39, 151
Congressional caucuses, 46, 47, 52
Congressional Government, 143
congressional presidency, 26, 28–31, 29
Constitutional Convention, 2, 3, 7, 9, 16, 31, 46; branches of government and, 26–27; elections and, 6–8; Federalists at, 4–5; on legislative role of president, 18–20; treaties and, 17–18; Twenty-second Amendment and, 148
Constitution of the United States, 11, 14, 29, 31, 34, 136; appointments and, 43; Electoral College and, 4, 45; on executive powers, 21; experimental quality of, 1–2, 35; political parties and, 52–53; separation of powers and, 8; signing of, 6
Consumer Protection Act, 123
Continental Congress, 2
Coolidge, Calvin, 60, 63, 64
Council of Economic Advisors (CEA), 94–95, 151
Council on Environmental Quality, 94–95
Crawford, William, 47
Cuban Missile Crisis, 141

D

Dayton Peace Accords, 125
death of president, 39, 57, 63, 79, 100
debt, 38, 87–88, 123, 164–65
deficits, 38, 72, 87, 88, 164–65
Democratic Party, 47, 59, 60, 91; elections and, 40, 61; orientation of, 54; primaries and, 50; against Republican Party, 53; split-party government and, 56
Democratic-Republicans, 46, 47, 53
Department of Defense, 67, 85, 90–91, 152, 153
Department of Health and Human Services, 67, 165
Department of Homeland Security, 85, 121, 165
Department of State, 93
Dickinson, John, 9
Domestic Policy Council, 95

D

economy, 37, 38, 73, 150, 151
Eisenhower, Dwight D., 35, 56, 69, 76, 132; expectations for, 40; Korean War and, 37; primaries and, 50; reelection of, 60; Social programs and, 37–38
elections, 7, 40, 43, 45; branches of government and, 5; Bush, G. W., and, 47, 61, 64; Carter and, 60, 61, 73; Congress and, 21, 54, 65; Constitutional Convention and, 6–8; House of Representatives and, 8, 21, 54–57; reelection of presidents, 9–11, 60. See also Electoral College.
Electoral College, 23, 42, 48, 53; Congress and, 7–8, 21, 44–45; Constitution of the Unites States and, 44, 45; House of Representatives and, 8, 21, 43–44, 45, 47; impeachment and, 11, 13; Twelfth Amendment and, 65; vice presidency and, 43–44. See also elections.
Elementary and Secondary Education Act, 134
Employment Act (1946), 95, 151
Executive Office of the President (EOP), 94, 95, 106, 151–152

executive power, 3–4, 5, 65; Article II and, 77, 85, 161; Constitution and, 21; definition of, 14–16; military and, 16–17; separation of powers and, 28, 78, 109, 158

F

Fair Deal, 38
Federal Bureau of Investigation (FBI), 76
Federal Election Campaign Act (1974), 152, 155
Federal Election Commission (FEC), 152
Federal employment, 86
Federal Hall, 23
Federalist, The, 5, 9–10, 12, 52
Federalists, 7, 43, 53; at Constitutional Convention, 4–5; decline of, 46–47, 142
Federal Reserve Act (1913), 151
Federal Reserve Board, 153
Federal Reserve System, 89–90
Federal Trade Commission, 81
Fifteenth Amendment, 147
First Amendment, 92, 155, 156
First Lady, 102–4, 160
Ford, Gerald, 40, 56, 59, 60, 63, 69
foreign policy, 6, 14, 17, 126
Founding Fathers, 1–3, 13, 42–43, 47, 83, 166; branches of government and, 20–22; elections and, 64–65; separated elections and, 54–55; separated presidency and, 31, 34, 54–55; separation of powers and, 54, 85, 109
Framers of the Constitution, 5, 13
Franklin, Benjamin, 1, 9, 46
Freedom of Information Act (1974), 152, 154

G

Gallup Poll, 57
Garfield, James, 56, 61
Gates, Robert, 69
Gingrich, Newt, 119, 132
Goldfine, Bernard, 81
Gonzalez, Alberto, 70
Gore, Al, 64, 100, 101
Government Accountability Office (GAO), 136
Gramm-Rudman-Hollings Anti-Deficit Act (1985), 151
Grant, Ulysses S., 56, 60
Gray, C. Boyden, 76
Great Depression, 37, 49, 155
Great Society program, 38, 113, 128, 134, 140
Guantanamo Bay, 111–12
Gulf of Mexico oil spill, 135–36

H

Hagel, Chuck, 89
Hamdan v. Rumsfeld, 156, 157
Hamilton, Alexander, 1, 5, 11–12, 31, 36, 46; on presidential presidency, 27, 28, 117; on term length, 9–10; on veto power, 18
Harrison, Benjamin, 56, 60, 61
Hayes, Rutherford B., 56, 61
health care: Clinton and, 39, 111, 119, 133; Obama and, 39, 122, 124, 140. *See also* Affordable Care Act.
Herring, E. Pendleton, 166
Holder, Eric, 70
Hoover, Herbert, 56, 60
House Committee on Armed Services, 91
House Committee on the Budget, 96
House Committee on Ways and Means, 133
House of Lords, 13

House of Representatives, 11, 12, 17, 35, 59, 86; elections and, 8, 21, 54–57; Electoral College and, 8, 21, 43–44, 45, 47; split-party government and, 55–57
Huitt, Ralph K., 112
Humphrey, Hubert, 50, 51, 101
Humphries Executor v. United States, 156, 157
Hurricane Katrina, 82, 121, 130–31, 135
Hurricane Sandy, 105
Hussein, Saddam, 130

I

immigration, 129, 131, 163–64
impeachment, 12, 21, 29, 30; Clinton and, 11, 13, 82, 119, 161; separation of powers and, 14
inauguration, *62*
independent agencies, 89
Independent Democratic-Republican Party, 53
Intelligence Overhaul (2004), 152
Internal Revenue Service (IRS), 14
Iran-contra scandal, 38, 81–82
Iraq, 82, 120, 121, 125, 126, 130

J

Jackson, Andrew, 36, 47, 48
Jay, John, 46
Jefferson, Thomas, 36, 43, 44, 46, 142
Jeffords, James, 120
Johnson, Andrew, 39, 59, 60, 69
Johnson, Lady Bird, 102
Johnson, Lyndon B., 60, 63, 64, 128; Congress and, 112–13; on fitting in, 39, 40; primaries and, 50; social programs of, 38; Vietnam War and, 132

Jones, Paula, 157
judiciary, 15, 21, 69, 90. *See also* Supreme Court.

K

Kefauver, Estes, 50
Kennedy, John F. (JFK), 39, 40, 61, 74–75, *76*
Kennedy, Robert, 50, 51
Khamenei, Ayatollah, 104
King Felipe VI, 104
King v. Burwell, 150
Korean War, 37, 156

L

lame duck president, 83, 108, 146
League of Nations, 72
legislative role of president, 18–20
L'Enfant, Major Pierre Charles, 24, *25*
Lewinsky, Monica, 38, 82, 119
Lincoln, Abraham, 35, 36, 60, 61
Lynch, Loretta, 70

M

Madison, Dolley, 102
Madison, James, 1, 17, 26, 46, 52, 53, 117
Marbury v. Madison, 136, 158
Marshall, John, 136
McCain, John, 43
McCarthy, Eugene, 50
McKinley, William, 35, 60, 61, 81, 142
media, 19, 34, 51, 52, 76, 89, 131; adversarial role of, 91–92; appointments and, 74; policy evaluation and, 106, 136–37, 154; polls and, 57, 59; primaries and, 51. *See also* communications.
Medicaid, 38, 87, 92, 127, 135
Medical Care for the Aged Act (1965), 128

Medicare, 38, 127, 128, 133, 135
military, 14, 16–17, 31, 87, 94, 106
Mills, Wilbur, 133
Mineta, Norman, 69
Mondale, Walter, 64, 100
Monroe, James, 26
Morris, Dick, 99
Myers v. United States, 156, 157

N

narrow-margin politics, 162
National Commission on Terrorist
    Attacks, 152
national defense, 127, 150
National Economic Council (1993),
    95, 153
National Environmental Protection
    Act (1969), 95
*National Federation of Independent
    Business v. Sebelius*, 150
National First Ladies Library
    (NFLL), 103
National Industrial Recovery Act, 155
National Narcotics Leadership Act
    (1988), 95
National Science and Technology
    Policy Organization and
    Priorities Act (1971), 95
national security, 114, 152, 163–64
National Security Act (1947), 95, 152
National Security Council (NSC),
    94, 95, 152, 153
NATO, 126
Neustadt, Richard E., 101, 103, 111,
    112, 143–44
New Deal, 37, 128
New Jersey Plan, 5, 6, 9
Nineteenth Amendment, 147
Nixon, Pat, 102
Nixon, Richard, 12, 27, 35, 56,
    61,69, 73; Congress and, 113;
    public mood and, 39; reelection
    of, 60; resignation of, 63, 79, 81,

156–57; social programs and, 38;
    Vietnam War and, 37; Watergate
    scandal and, 38, 40, 81
No Child Left Behind, 120
North American Free Trade
    Agreement, 118–19

O

Obama, Barack, 27, *33*, 35, 38, 39,
    43, 56, 61,74, 117; Affordable
    Care Act/Obamacare and, 68, 83,
    92, 122–23, 149–50, 165;
    appointments of, 70; background
    of, 114; enactments of, 116; Great
    Recession and, 38, 74; on
    Guantanamo Bay, 111–12; health
    care and, 39, 124, 140; historic
    presidency of, 117, 122–25; polls
    and, 58; reelection of, 60; vice
    presidency and, 64
Obama, Michelle, 103
Obamacare. *See* Affordable Care
    Act; health care.
Office of Administration, 95, 96
Office of Management and Budget
    (OMB), 94, 95, 96, 136, 137,
    138, 139
Office of National Drug Control
    Policy, 95–96
Office of Policy Development, 95
Office of Science and Technology
    Policy, 94–95
Office of the First Lady, 102
Office of the US Trade
    Representative, 95–96
Office of the Vice President, 95
omnibus crime law, 119
O'Neill, Paul, 89

P

parliamentary system, 7, 29, 30, 54, 78
Patriot Act, 134

Patterson, Bradley H., 96, 99
Pendleton Act (1883), 68
Pinckney, Thomas, 46
polarization, 161–62
policies, 132; implementation of,
    135, 136; incremental
    adjustments of, 127–28;
    legitimation of, 133; major
    overhauls of, 127, 128–29; option
    formulation of, 133; in split-party
    government, 117; substance of,
    115–25, 124; on terrorism, 116,
    120–21, 125–26, 131. *See also*
    foreign policy.
political parties, 52–53, 60
polls, 57–59, 65, 99
Pope Francis, 105–6
popular election, 42, 44
popular vote, 7, 47, 59, 61, 63, 65;
    appointments in, 69; executive
    power and, 17; policies and, 132;
    split-party government and 55,
    166; term lengths in, 35
Powell, Colin, 70
presidential presidency, 26, 27,
    28, 117
President's Committee on
    Administrative Management, 94
press secretary, 92, 106
primaries, 48–50
Progressives, 142
Putin, Vladimir, 106
Putting People First campaign,
    118

Q

Quayle, Dan, 101
Queen Elizabeth, 104

R

Randolph, Edmund, 36
Reagan, Nancy, 102, 103

Reagan, Ronald, 35, 36, 56, 61, 71,
    73; Congress and, 113; diversity
    and, 70; Iran-Contra scandal
    and, 38; public expectations for,
    39; reelection of, 60; transition
    of, 74–75, 100
recession, 36, 38, 74, 82, 83, 122
Reciprocal Trade Agreement Act
    (1934), 151
Reedy, George E., 106–7
reforms, 38, 152, 164; of
    amendments, 146–49; of budget,
    150, 151; separation of powers
    and, 144, 145; as statutes,
    149–50; Supreme Court and,
    155–58; Vice presidency and,
    146–48
Rehnquist, William H., 11
Reno, Janet, 70
Reorganization Plan (1939), 151
Republican party, 46, 47, 56, 59, 60,
    61, 91; against Democratic Party,
    53; nominations by, 49; orientation
    of, 54; primaries and, 50
Residency Act, 24
Rice, Condoleezza, 70
Road Map to Peace Initiative, 126
Rockefeller, Nelson, 147
Romney, Mitt, 43
Roosevelt, Eleanor, 103
Roosevelt, Franklin D. (FDR), 11,
    27, 35, 36, 59; with Churchill,
    159; Congress and, 37; primaries
    and, 49; public expectations for,
    39; reelection of, 60; social
    programs of, 37–38
Roosevelt, Theodore, 27, 36, 63, 66
Rove, Karl, 99

S

scandal, 38, 40, 81–82, 83
*Schechter Poultry Corporation v.
    United States*, 155

second-term appointments, 81–82, 83

secretary of state, 47, 104

Senate, 13, 27, 29, 30, 59, 86; elections and, 9–11, 54–57; Electoral College and, 43–44; separated presidency and, 31, 32, 54–57; separation of powers and, 109; split-party government and, 55–57; treaties and, 17, 21, 28, 31

Senate Committee on Armed Services, 91

Senate Committee on the Budget, 96

separated presidency, 26–27, 28; Constitutional Convention and, 31–34; Madison on, 52–53, 117; Senate and, 31, 32, 54–57

separating to unify, 2

separation of elections, 53, 54–57, 124

separation of powers, 2, 3, 4, 6, 7, 8, 14, 16, 21, 67, 83, 84, 105, 110, 141; appointments and, 16; congressional presidency and, 30, 31; deformation of, 124, 163; elections and, 5, 54, 57, 65; executive powers and, 28, 78, 109, 158; historical presidents and, 124; Madison on, 52, 53, 117; reforms and, 144, 145; Senate and Supreme Court, 109; statutes and, 154; treaty making and, 17–18. *See also* branches of government; separated presidency.

Seventeenth Amendment, 12, 65

Skowronek, Stephen, 37

Social Security, 39, 82, 121, 127, 128, 129

Souter, David, 90

split-party government, 27, 56, 58, 110–11, 118, 139; appointments and, 77, 90; Congress and, 55, 63; enactments of, 116; House of Representatives and, 55–57; policies in, 117; polls and, 58; post-World War II and, 55, 166; Senate and, 55–57

Starr, Kenneth, 82

State of the Union address, 32, 33, 105, 132; by Clinton, 111, 114, 119; development of, 19, 21

Stevens, John Paul, 90

Stevenson, Adlai, 50

Suffrage, 148

Supreme Court, 29, 30, 32, 109; appointments and, 15, 31, 35, 77; cases of, 157; on impeachment, 13; reforms and, 155–58. *See also* judiciary.

T

Taft, Robert A., 50, 56, 60, 61

Taft, William Howard, 105

Task Force on National Health Care Reform, 103–4

Taxes, 72, 73, 119, 123

term length, 29, 30, 42, 55, 65; Constitutional Convention and, 7; debate over, 6, 9–11; Hamilton on, 9–10; Influence of, 54; in judiciary, 90; Madison on, 53; in post-World War II, 35

terrorism, 37, 154–55, 163; Bush, G. W., campaign and, 72; policies and, 116, 120–21, 125–26, 131

Tower, John, 77

Travel of presidents, 49, 71, 72, 105, 114, 159–60

treason, impeachment for, 12

treasurer, 27, 29, 30, 47

treaties, 17–18, 21, 28, 29, 30, 32

Truman, Harry S., 36, 56, 110, 128; election, 60, 61; on fitting in, 39, 40; Roosevelt, FDR, and, 49; scandal and, 38; social programs of, 38; as successor 64, 66; World War II and, 37

Twelfth Amendment, 43, 45, 47, 65, 146, 147

Twentieth Amendment, 147
Twenty-fifth Amendment, 32, 146, 147, 148
Twenty-fourth Amendment, 147
Twenty-second Amendment, 11, 35, 78–79, 145, 147, 148
Twenty-sixth Amendment, 147
Twenty-third Amendment, 146, 147

U

United States Government Manual, 85
United States v. Butler, 155
United States v. Nixon, 157
Use of Force Resolution, 125

V

Van Buren, Martin, 101
veto power, 18–19, 21, 27, 31, 32
vice presidency, 8, 32, 63, 66, 101–2; Carter and, 64; Congress and, 21; Electoral College and, 43–44; Obama and, 64; reforms and, 146–48; role of, 64, 100, 160
Vietnam War, 37, 50, 73, 126, 132, 140
Virginia Plan, 5, 6, 15, 18, 29–30, 29

W

Wall Street reform, 122–23
War, 16–17, 29, 30, 31, 36, 37

War Powers Act (1973), 38, 152, 154
Washington, George, 1, 3–4, 11, 25, 27, 44; Electoral College and, 44; Madison and, 36; signing Constitution, 6; trial presidency of, 35, 42; two-term precedent of, 11, 34–35, 43
Watergate scandal, 38, 40, 81, 155, 156–57
Welfare, 119, 129
West Wing, 98
Whig Party, 53
White, Byron, 90
White House, 26, 36, 98, 105, 160
White House Office (WHO), 94, 95, 96
Wills, Gary, 91
Wilson, Woodrow, 27, 36, 56, 60, 61, 72, 81, 143
World Trade Center, 105, 120, 130
World War II, 37, 49, 50
Wright, James, 132

X

Xi Jinping, 105–6

Y

Youngstown Sheet & Tube Co. v. Sawyer, 157